THE

DOMESTIC SLAVE TRADE

OF THE

SOUTHERN STATES

BY

WINFIELD H. COLLINS, M. A.

Professor of History and English in Claremont College.

BROADWAY PUBLISHING
COMPANY :: AT 835
BROADWAY NEW YORK

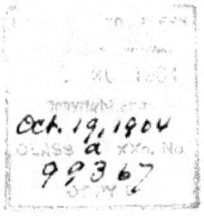

PREFACE.

WHEN I began the study of the Domestic Slave Trade of the Southern States I had no idea of the conclusions as herein found. Especially is this true of Chapters III. and IV. I have spared no pains to be accurate in all statements of fact.

The material for this work was collected in the Yale University Library in New Haven, Connecticut, and in the Congressional Library at Washington. The sources used are to be found in the appended bibliography. The most helpful were books of travel, newspapers and periodicals, Statistics of Southern States and the United States Census Reports.   W. H. COLLINS.

Claremont College,

Hickory, N. C.

February 22, 1904.

CONTENTS

THE DOMESTIC SLAVE TRADE
OF THE
SOUTHERN STATES.

CHAPTER I.

A SKETCH OF THE RISE OF THE SLAVE TRADE IN AFRICAN STATES AND OF THE FOREIGN SLAVE TRADE OF THE SOUTHERN STATES.

IT is not our intention nor is it within our province to enter into details concerning the foreign slave trade. It seems, however, that a brief account is necessary as introductory to the subject of the Domestic Slave Trade.

The rise in Europe of the traffic in slaves from Africa was an incident in the commercial expansion of Portugal. It was coeval and almost coextensive with the development of commerce, and followed in the wake of discovery and colonization.

The first name connected with it is that of
Antonio Gonçalvez, who was a marine under
Prince Henry the Navigator. In 1441 he was
sent to Cape Bojador to get a vessel load of "sea-
wolves" skins. He signalized his voyage by the
capture of some Moors whom he carried to Portugal. In 1442 these Moors promised black
slaves as a ransom for themselves. Prince Henry
approved of this exchange and Gonçalvez took
the captives home and received, among other
things, ten black slaves in exchange for two of
them. The king justified his act on the ground
that the negroes might be converted to the
Christian religion, but the Moors could not.[1]
Two years later the Company of Lagos chartered
by the king, and engaged in exploration on the
coast of Africa, imported about two hundred
slaves from the islands of Nar and Tidar.[2]
"This year (1444) Europe may be said to have
made a distinct beginning in the slave trade,
henceforth to spread on all sides like the waves

---

[1]A. Helps: The Spanish Conquest of America, Vol.
I., 30-32.

[2]Ibid., 35-36.

[in] stirred up water, and not like them to become fainter and fainter as the circles widen."[3]

After the discovery of America, the islands
which became known as the Spanish West Indies were speedily colonized, and the inefficiency
of the Indian as a laborer in the mines there soon
led to the substitution of the negro. As early
as 1502 a few were employed, and in 1517 Charles
V. granted a patent to certain traders for the
exclusive supply of 4,000 negroes annually to the
islands of Hispaniola, Cuba, Jamaica and Porto
Rico.[4]

So far as known John Hawkins was the first
Englishman to engage in the slave traffic.   He
left England for Sierra Leone with three ships
and a hundred men in 1562, and having secured
three hundred negroes he proceeded to Hispaniola where he disposed of them, and having
had a very profitable voyage, he returned to
England in 1563. This appears to have excited
the avarice of the British Government. The next

---

[3]Helps: Sp. Con. of Am., Vol. I., 40.
[4]Edwards: British West Indies, Vol. II., 44.
Brock: Va. Hist. So. Collection, Vol. VI., 2.

year Hawkins was appointed to the command of
one of the Queen's ships and proceeded to Africa
where in company with several others, it appears,
he engaged in the slave traffic.[5]

In 1624 France began the slave trade and later
Holland, Denmark, New England and other
English colonies, though the leader in the trade
and the last to abandon it was Great Britain.[6]

The first slaves introduced into any of the English continental colonies was in 1619 about the
last of August when a piratical Dutch frigate,
manned chiefly by English, stopped at James-
town, Virginia, and sold the colonists twenty
negroes.[7]   Even for a long while after this, it
seems, importation of negroes was merely of an
occasional or incidental nature.   Indeed, in 1648
only three hundred negroes were to be found
in Virginia.[8]   However, several shiploads were

[5]Edwards: British West Indies, Vol. II., 47-8.

[6]Ballaugh: Hist. of Slavery in Va., p. 4.

[7]John Smith: Hist. of Va., Vol. II., 39.
Ballaugh: Hist. of Slavery in Va., pp. 8-9.   There
has been some misunderstanding as to the date, but
Ballaugh makes it clear that 1619 is correct.

[8]Brock: Va. Hist. So. Coll., VI., 9.
Ballaugh: Hist. Sl. in Va., p. 9.

brought in between 1664 and 1671, and at the latter date Virginia had two thousand slaves.[9] During the latter part of the seventeenth and the early part of the eighteenth century the importation of negroes gradually increased. In 1705, eighteen hundred negroes were brought in and in 1715 Virginia had twenty-three thousand. By 1723 they were being imported into this colony at the rate of fifteen hundred or sixteen hundred a year.[10]

In the eighteenth century Virginia sought from time to time to hinder the introduction of slaves by placing heavy duties on them. Indeed, from 1732 until the Revolution there were only about six months in which slaves could be brought into Virginia free of duty.[11] Nevertheless, in 1776 Virginia had 165,000 slaves.[12]

Though all the other colonies imported slaves more or less during the same period, yet with

[9]Hening: States at Large, Vol. II., 515.

[10]Ballaugh: Hist. Sl. in Va., pp. 10-14.

[11]Ibid., p. 19.

[12]De Bow: Industrial Resources of the South, Vol. III., 130.

the possible exception of South Carolina they fell far short of the number imported by Virginia.

In November 1708, Governor Seymour of Maryland, writing to the English Board of Trade, stated that 2,290 negroes were imported into that colony from midsummer 1698 to Christmas 1707. He reported the trade to be running very high, six or seven hundred having been imported during the year. In 1712 there were 8,330 negroes in Maryland.[13] During about the same time (midsummer 1699 to October 1708) Virginia imported 6,607[14] while a northern colony, New Jersey, imported only one hundred and fifteen from 1698 to 1726.[15]

Du Bois says that South Carolina received about three thousand slaves a year from 1733 to 1766.[16] She had forty thousand in 1740.[17]

In 1700 North Carolina had eleven hundred,

---

[13]Scharf: Hist. of Md., Vol. I., 376-7.

[14]N. C. Colonial Records, Vol. I., 693.

[15]N. J. Archives, Vol. V., 152.

[16]Du Bois: Suppression of Slave Trade, p. 5.

[17]M'Call: Hist. of Ga., II., 125.

1732 six thousand,[18] and in 1764 about thirty thousand.[19]

Until near the beginning of the eighteenth century it was rare that the English continental colonies received a shipload of slaves direct from Africa, and even these were usually brought in by some unlicensed "interloper." It is very probable that most of the negroes imported before this time were from Barbados, Jamaica and other West India Islands.[20] But by the beginning of the eighteenth century it appears that slaves were being imported more rapidly. After the Assiento,[21] in 1713, England became a great carrier of slaves and so continued until the Revolution.[22] The effect of this was very sensibly felt by the colonies.

Even in the latter part of the seventeenth cen-

---

[18]N. C. Colonial Records, Vol. II., p. 17.

[19]Bassett: Slavery and Servitude in N. C., pages 20-22. In J. H. U. Studies, Vol. XIV.

[20]Scharf: Hist. of Md., Vol. I., 376-7.
N. C. Colonial Records, Vol. I., 693.

[21]The Assiento was a treaty between England and Spain, by which Spain granted England a monopoly of the Spanish colonial slave trade for thirty years. Du Bois: Suppression of Slave Trade, p. 3.

[22]Du Bois: Suppression of Slave Trade, p. 4-6.

tury some of the colonies began to show their dislike by levying duties on further importation. In
the eighteenth century the colonial opposition to
the importation of slaves, arising probably from a
fear of insurrection, became much more pro-
nounced. Heavy restrictions in the form of duties
were laid upon the trade. In some cases these
were so heavy as would seem to amount to total
prohibition.[23]   But the efforts on the part of the
colonies to restrict the trade were frowned upon
and often disallowed by the British Government.[24]

In 1754 the instructions to Governor Dobbs, of
North Carolina, were: "Whereas, acts have been
passed in some of our plantations in America
for laying duties on the importation and exportation of negroes to the great discouragement of
the Merchants trading thither from the coast of
Africa, . . . it is our will and pleasure that
you do not give your assent to or pass any law
imposing duties upon negroes imported into our
Province of North Carolina."[25]

[23]Du Bois: Suppression of Slave Trade, Appendix A.
[24]Ibid., pp. 4-5.
[25]N. C. Col. Rec., Vol. V., 1118.

The colonies considered the slave trade so important to Great Britain that at the dawn of the Revolution some of them appear to have had hopes of bringing her to terms by refusing to import any more slaves.[26]

In the original draft of the Declaration of Independence as submitted by Jefferson, the king of Great Britain is arraigned "for suppressing every legislative attempt to prohibit or restrain this execrable commerce."[27]

It has been estimated that in the year of the Declaration the whole number of slaves in the thirteen colonies was 502,132, apportioned as follows: Massachusetts, 3,500; Rhode Island, 4,376; Connecticut, 6,000; New Hampshire, 627; New York, 15,000; New Jersey, 7,600; Pennsylvania, 10,000; Delaware, 9,000; Maryland, 80,000; Georgia, 16,000; North Carolina, 75,-000; South Carolina, 110,000; Virginia, 165,-000.[28]

---

[26]Du Bois: Suppression of Slave Trade, pp. 42-8.

[27]Ford: Jefferson's Works, Vol. II., 23.

[28]De Bow's: Industrial Resources, Vol. III., 130. Liberator: Feb. 23, 1849.

Two years after this, in 1778, Virginia took the lead against the introduction of slaves by passing a law prohibiting importation either by land or sea. This law made an exception of travellers and immigrants.[29]   Other States soon followed suit, passing laws to restrict it temporarily or at specified places.[30]   By 1803 all the States and territories had laws in force prohibiting the importation of slaves from abroad.[31]   It must not be supposed, however, that these were entirely effective. Indeed, the statement was made in Congress Feb. 14, 1804, that in the preceding twelve months "twenty thousand" enslaved negroes had been transported from Guinea, and by smuggling, added to the plantation stock of Georgia and South Carolina.[32]

In 1798 an act of Congress establishing the territory of Mississippi provided that no slave should be brought within its limits from without

[29]Hening: Statutes at Large, Vol. IX., p. 471.

[30]Chap. on Laws. C. VII., this book.
    Du Bois: Suppres. Sl. Trade, Appendices A. and B.
[31]Ibid.
    Schouler: Hist. U. S., Vol. II., p. 56.
    Chap. VII. on Laws, this volume.
[32]Annals of Congress, 8th Cong., 1st Sess., 1000.

the United States.[33]   In 1804, when Louisiana
was erected into the territories of Louisiana and
Orleans the provision was made that only slaves
which had been imported before May 1, 1798,
might be introduced into the territories and these
must be the bona fide property of actual settlers.[34]

Upon the petition of the inhabitants for the
removal of the restrictions, a bill was introduced
in Congress, of which Du Bois says: "By dexter-
ous wording, this bill, which became a law March
2, 1805, swept away all restrictions upon the slave
trade except that relating to foreign ports, and
left even this provision so ambiguous that later
by judicial interpretations of the law, the foreign
slave trade was allowed at least for a time."[35]

South Carolina had even before this time (December 17, 1803), repealed her law against the importation of slaves from Africa.[36] The trade was
thus open through this State for four years, dur-

---

[33]Poore: Fed. and State Constitutions, Part 2, 1050.
[34]Ibid.

[35]Du Bois: Suppression of Slave Trade, pp. 89-90.
[36]McCord: S. C. Statutes at Large, Vol. VII., p. 449.
Du Bois: p. 240.

ing which time 39,075 slaves were imported through Charleston[37] alone.

The action of South Carolina in opening the slave trade forced the question upon the attention of Congress. During 1805-6 it was much discussed[38] but it was not until March 2, 1807, that a bill was passed against it. This prohibited the importation of slaves after January 1, 1808, under penalty of imprisonment for not less than five nor more than ten years, and a fine of not less than $5,000 nor more than $10,000.[39]

This law was not entirely effective. In 1810 the Secretary of the Navy writing to Charleston, South Carolina, says: "I hear not without great concern, that the law prohibiting the importation of slaves has been violated in frequent instances near St. Mary's."[40]

Drake, a slave smuggler, says, that during the war of 1812 the business of smuggling slaves

---

[37]Annals of Congress, 16 Con., 2nd Sess., p. 77.
[38]Du Bois: pp. 91-3.
[39]Annals of Cong., 9 Cong., 2 Sess., Appendix 1266-72.
[40]House Doc., 15 Cong., 2 Sess., IV., No. 84, p. 5.

through Florida into the United States was a
lively one.[41]

Vincent Nolte says that in 1813 "pirates cap-
tured Spanish and other slave ships on the high
seas and established their main depot and rendez-
vous on the island of Barataria lying near
the coast adjacent to New Orleans.   This place
was visited by the sugar planters, chiefly of
French origin, who bought up the stolen slaves
at from $150 to $200 per head when they could
not have procured as good stock in the city for less
than $600 or $700.   These were then conveyed
to the different plantations, through the innu-
merable creeks called bayous, that communicate
with each other by manifold little branches."[42]

In 1817-1819 slaves were very high and in great
demand in the South.   As a consequence great
numbers of them were smuggled in at various
places.   The evidence of this is quite convincing.

Amelia Island and the town of St. Mary's became notorious as two of the principal rendez-

[41]Drake: Revelations of a Slave Smuggler, 51, quoted
by Du Bois, p. 11.

[42]Vincent Nolte: Fifty Years in Both Hemispheres,
p. 189.

vous of smugglers. A writer in "Niles' Register"
in 1818 says that a regular chain of posts was
established from the head of St. Mary's river to
the upper country, and through the Indian nation by means of which slaves are hurried to every
part of the country. The woodmen along the
river side rode like so many Arabs loaded with
slaves ready for market. When ready to form a
caravan, an Indian alarm was created that the
woods might be less frequented, and if pursued
in Georgia they escaped to Florida.[43]

Mr. M'Intosh, Collector of the Port of Darien,
in a letter in 1818, says: "I am in possession of
undoubted information that African and West
Indian negroes are almost daily illicitly introduced into Georgia, for sale or settlement, or
passing through it to the territories of the United
States."[44]

In 1817 it was reported to the Secretary of the
Navy that "most of the goods carried to Galveston are introduced into the United States, the most

---

[43]Niles' Reg., May 2, 1818.

[44]State Papers, 1st Sess., 16th Cong., Vol. 3, H.
Doc. 42.

bulky and least valuable regularly through the custom house; the most valuable and the slaves are smuggled in through the numerous inlets to the westward where the people are but too much disposed to render them every possible assistance. Several hundred slaves are now at Galveston."[45]

"Niles' Register," in 1818, quoting from the "Democrat Press," has a very interesting account of how the law against the importation of slaves was evaded at New Orleans: An agent would be sent to the West Indies and even to Africa to purchase a cargo of slaves. On the return when the slave ship got near Balize the agent would leave her, go in haste to New Orleans and inform the proper authorities that a certain vessel had come into the Mississippi, said to be bound for New Orleans and having on board a certain number of negroes contrary to the law of the United States. The vessel and cargo would be libelled and the slaves sold at public auction. One half of the purchase money would go to the informer and the other to the United States.[46]　The in-

---

[45]Niles' Reg., Jan. 22, 1820.
[46]Ibid., Dec. 12, 1818, Louisiana had a law which

former and agent was the same man and a part-
ner in the transaction. This was a profitable
business and about ten thousand slaves a year are
said to have been thus introduced.[47]

It is quite evident that the illicit slave trade
at this time was very great. In 1819 Mr. Middle-
ton, of South Carolina, said in Congress that in
his opinion thirteen thousand Africans were annually smuggled into the United States, and Mr.
Wright, of Virginia, estimated the number at fifteen thousand.[48]

In 1818, 1819 and 1820 Congress passed acts to
supplement and render more effective the act of
1807.[49] Du Bois says that for a decade after 1825
there appears little positive evidence of a large illicit importation, but thinks notwithstanding that
slaves were largely imported.[50]

Captain J. E. Alexander in a book published

provided that slaves imported contrary to Act of Congress, March 2, 1807, should be seized and sold for
benefit of the State. (Hurd, Vol. II., p. 159.) But the
whole story is denied by another writer. (Niles' Reg.,
Dec. 12, 1818.)

[47]Niles' Reg., Dec. 12, 1818.
[48]Wm. Jay: Miscell. Writings on Slavery, p. 277.
[49]Du Bois: Pp. 118-122.
[50]Ibid., p. 128.

in 1833 says that he was assured by a planter of
forty years' standing that persons in New Orleans
were connected with slave traders in Cuba, and
that at certain seasons of the year they would go
up the Mississippi River and meet slave ships off
the coast. They would relieve these of their cargoes, return to the main stream of the river, drop
down in flat boats and dispose of the negroes to
those who wished them.[51] Thomas Powell Buxton makes the statement, upon what he claims
to be high authority, that fifteen thousand negroes were imported into Texas from Africa in
one year, about 1838.[52]

The "Liberator" quoting the "Maryland Colonization Herald," says a writer in that paper was
assured, in 1838, by Pedro Blanco, one of the
largest slave traders on the coast of Africa, that
for the preceding forty years the United States
had been his best market through the west end
of Cuba and Texas.[53]

"Between 1847 and 1853," says Du Bois, "the

---

[51]Alexander: Transatlantic Sketches, p. 230.
[52]Buxton: The African Slave Trade, p. 44.
[53]Liberator: Aug. 18, 1854.

slave smuggler Drake had a slave depot in the Gulf, where sometimes as many as sixteen hundred negroes were on hand, and the owners were continually importing and shipping."

Drake himself says: "Our island was visited almost weekly by agents from Cuba, New York, Baltimore, Philadelphia, Boston and New Orleans, . . . the seasoned and instructed slaves were taken to Texas or Florida, overland, and to Cuba, in sailing boats. As no squad contained more than half a dozen, no difficulty was found in posting them to the United States, without discovery, and generally without suspicion. . . . The Bay Island plantation sent ventures weekly to the Florida Keys. Slaves were taken into the great American swamps, and there kept till wanted for market. Hundreds were sold as runaways from the Florida wilderness. We had agents in every slave State, and our coasters were built in Maine and came out with lumber. I could tell curious stories . . . of this business of smuggling Bozal negroes into the United States. It is growing more profitable every year, and if you should hang all the Yankee merchants engaged in it, hundreds would fill their places."[54]

Owing to the increasing demand, and to the high price of slaves from 1845 to 1860, and to the fact that the Southern people were becoming more and more favorable to the reopening of the African slave trade, thus making it easier to practice smuggling successfully, we have no reason to doubt the truth of these accounts of this illicit traffic.

Stephen A. Douglas said in 1859 it was his confident opinion that more than fifteen thousand slaves had been imported in the preceding year, and that the trade had been carried on extensively for a long while.[55] About 1860 it was stated that twenty large cities and towns in the South were depots for African slaves and sixty or seventy cargoes of slaves had been introduced in the preceding eighteen months.[56] It was estimated in 1860 that eighty-five vessels which had been fitted out from New York City during eigh-

---

[54]Revelations of a Slave Smuggler, p. 98.   Quoted by Du Bois, p. 166.

[55]27 Report Am. Anti-Slavery So., p. 20.
Du Bois: P. 181.

[56]27 Report Am. Anti-Sl. So., p. 21.   Du Bois, p. 182.

teen months of 1859 and 1860, would introduce from thirty thousand to sixty thousand annually.[57]

From what has been said it seems to us certain that at least 270,000 slaves were introduced into the United States from 1808 to 1860 inclusive.[58] These we would distribute as follows: Between 1808 and 1820, sixty thousand; 1820 to 1830, fifty thousand; 1830 to 1840, forty thousand; 1840 to 1850, fifty thousand and from 1850 to 1860 seventy thousand. We consider these very moderate and even low estimates.

It will be seen later that these figures are of prime importance in accounting for the presence of certain slaves in the States of the extreme South.

---

[57]J. J. Lalor: Cyclopedia, Vol. III., p. 733.

[58]This is little more than the estimate which Du Bois made before he wrote his book. "Suppression of the Slave Trade." "From 1807 to 1862 there were annually introduced into the United States from 1,000 to 15,000 Africans, and that the total number thus brought in in contravention alike of humanity and law was not less than 250,000." "Enforcement of Slave Trade Laws," in the Annual Report of the Am. Hist. Assoc. for the year 1801. p. 173. The estimate of 270,000 in the text was made after careful study, and before the writer knew of Du Bois' estimate.

CHAPTER II.

THE CAUSES OF THE RISE AND DEVELOPMENT OF THE DOMESTIC SLAVE TRADE.

THE prohibition of the foreign slave trade by
the States and the Federal Government is the first
thing to be considered in connection with the development of the internal slave trade. Although
before 1808 all the States had passed laws to
prohibit the introduction of slaves from without
the United States, yet each State had the power
to reopen the trade at will. South Carolina, perhaps, thinking it might be for the interest of the
State, opened the foreign trade in 1803.[1] During
the four years following so many slaves were imported that the market in the United States became overstocked and many of the negroes were
sent to the West Indies for sale.[2] Had the States

---

[1]McCord: S. C. Statutes at Large, Vol. VII., p. 449.
[2]Annals of Congress, 16 Cong., 2 Sess., p. 77.

retained the power to import, it is not probable
that the domestic trade would ever have assumed
any great importance.   It is not likely that the
people of the South and West would have paid
high prices for the negroes from the border
States when they could have been had from
abroad for so much less.

The great profits, too, which induced men to
carry on the domestic trade would have been
wanting.   Assuming this, then, the consequent
low price of slaves in the border slave States,
added to the disinclination of many in these States
to make merchandise of the negro, might have led,
as the negroes increased and became a burden
upon their masters, to gradual emancipation.

In 1807, however, when Congress exercised its
constitutional right and prohibited the importation
of slaves from without the United States after
January 1, 1808, the right of the individual States
to import slaves from foreign countries was lost.

It is interesting to note that only a few years
before the passage of the Federal non-importa-
tion-slave act the vast territory of Louisiana had
been purchased from France.   The acquisition of

this territory had a wonderful influence upon the
development and continuance of the internal slave
trade.

Of much less influence, and we might even say,
of comparative insignificance, was the Florida cession of 1819. In a very short time this fertile region of the Louisiana purchase began to attract
great numbers of immigrants who, it seems, often
brought their slaves with them. But there were
many who still had to be supplied.[3] To meet this
demand recourse was had, principally, to the exhausted plantations of Virginia and Maryland.[4]

Tobacco, which had been a great agricultural
staple in these States, had worn out the land. The
price of tobacco, too, from about 1818 was very
low and continued so until about 1840.[5] At the
same time new States such as Kentucky, Tennessee, Missouri, the Carolinas and Georgia, had become great tobacco States. Such quantities came
to be raised as to make the culture very un-

[3](Ingraham) : The Southwest, Vol. II., p. 223.
[4]Alexander: Transatlantic Sketches, p. 250.
Basil Hall: Travels in N. Am., Vol. II., p. 217.
[5]Hunt's: Merchants' Magazine, Vol. VI., p. 473.

profitable in Virginia and Maryland.[6] The con‑
dition with respect to this section could be no bet‑
ter illustrated than by a quotation from a speech
of Thomas Marshall in the Virginia House of
Delegates, January 20, 1832:

"Mr. Taylor, of Carolina," he says, "had under‑
stood that 60,000 hogsheads of tobacco were ex‑
ported from Virginia, when the whole population
did not exceed 150,000. Had the fertility of the
country by possibility remained undiminished,
Virginia ought in 1810 to have exported 240,000
hogsheads, or their equivalent in other produce,
and at present nearly double that. Thus the agri‑
cultural exports of Virginia in 1810 would, at the
estimated prices of the Custom House at that time,
have been seventeen millions of dollars and now at
least thirty-four, while it is known that they are
not of late years greater than from three to five
millions. . . .

"The fact that the whole agricultural products
of the State at present, do not exceed in value the

[6]Speech of Thomas Marshall in Va., H. Del., 1832.
Richmond Enquirer, Feb. 2, 1832.

exports eighty or ninety years ago, when it contained not a sixth of the population, and when
not a third of the surface of that State (at present
Virginia) was at all occupied, is, however, a strik-
ing proof of the decline of its agriculture. What
is now the productive value of an estate of land
and negroes in Virginia? We state as the result
of extensive inquiry, embracing the last fifteen
years, that a very great proportion of the larger
plantations, with from fifty to one hundred slaves,
actually bring their proprietors in debt at the end
of a short term of years, notwithstanding what
would once in Virginia have been deemed very
sheer economy, that much the larger part of the
considerable landholders are content, if they
barely meet their plantation expenses without a
loss of capital; and that of those who make any
profit, it will be none but rare instances, average
more than one and a half per cent. on the capital
invested.   The case is not materially varied with
the smaller proprietors. Mr. Randolph, of Roa-
noke, whose sayings have so generally the raciness
and the truth of proverbs, has repeatedly said in
Congress, that the time was coming when the mas-

ters would run away from the slaves and be advertised by them in the public papers."[7]

It seems that agriculture had taken a new start
about 1816, probably owing to the fact that tobacco was very high, being from 8 to 15 cents per
pound,[8] for Colonel Mercer in the Virginia Constitutional Convention of 1829 said that in 1817
the lands of Virginia were valued at $206,000,000
and that negroes averaged $300 each, while by
1829 lands had decreased in value to $80,000,000
or $90,000,000 and negroes to $150 each.[9]   But
while agriculture was in such a discouraging condition in the worn out States, Louisiana and other
States of the Southwest were being opened up
and were looked on as the land of promise.   Immigrants to that favored section wrote glowing
accounts of the fertility of the country and of the
delightful climate.   An emigrant from Maryland
writes from Louisiana in 1817:

"Do not the climate, the soil and productions

[7]Richmond Enquirer, Feb. 2, 1832.

[8]Hunt's: Merchants' Magazine, VI., p. 473.

[9]Proceedings and Debate of the Va. St. Con. Con.,
1829-30, p. 178.

of this country furnish allurements to the appli-
cation of your negroes on our lands? In your
States a planter, with ten negroes, with difficulty
supports a family genteelly; here well managed,
they would be a fortune to him. With you the
seasons are so irregular your crops often fail;
here the crops are certain, and want of the neces-
saries of life, never for a moment causes the heart
to ache—abundance spreads the table of the poor
man and contentment smiles on every countenance."[10]

In marked contrast to the unprofitableness of
slave labor in the older slave States was their
immense profit when employed on the fresh lands
of the Southwest. Some planters in this section
had plantations thousands of acres in extent.[11] To
cultivate them great numbers of slaves were required. If the crop were cotton one negro was
needed for every three acres and these would
yield cotton to the value of $240 to $260. The
master realized upon each negro employed at least

[10]Niles' Reg., Sept. 13, 1817; for another such letter
see Ibid., October 18, 1817.

[11]Smedes: Memorials of a Southern Planter, p. 47.

$200 annually.[12]   The income of some of these
plantations was immense.   It was not uncommon
for a planter in Mississippi and Louisiana to have
an income of $30,000, and some of them even
$80,000 to $120,000 (1820).[13]

The enormous profits caused slaves to be very
high in this section and in great demand.   There
were only two possible sources of supply:—first,
the illicit traffic already spoken of; second, the
domestic slave trade.   A good negro from twenty
to thirty years of age would command from $800
to $1,200.[14]   Indeed, it is stated that at one time
during this early period they sold for as much as
$2,000.[15]   This fact in connection with the fact
that in 1817 the average price of a negro in Virginia was only $300, and the depreciation by 1829
to $150, gives us the reason for the rise of the

---

[12]Christian Scutz: Travels on an Inland Voyage, Vol.
II., p. 186.
    David Blowe: Geographical, Commercial and Agri-
cultural View of U. S., p. 618

[13]David Blowe: Geographical, Commercial and Agricultural View of U. S. of Am., p. 643.   (1820?)

[14]Ibid, p. 618.

[15]Claiborne: Miss. as a Province, Territory and State,
Vol. I., p. 144.

domestic slave trade.   It was over and again
stated in the Virginia Legislature of 1832 that the
value of negroes in Virginia was regulated not
by their profitableness at home but by the Southwestern demand.[16]   The great difference in the
price of slaves in the buying States and the selling States was an inducement to a certain class
of men to engage in the business of buying them
up and carrying them South.   The profits were
from one-third to one-half on an average after
expenses were paid.[17]   Slave traders soon got rich.
Williams, a Washington dealer, boasted in 1850
that he made $30,000 in a few months.[18]   It is
said the firm of Franklin & Armfield, of Alexandria, made $33,000 in 1829.[19]   In 1834 Armfield,
of this same firm, was reputed to be worth nearly
$500,000 which he had accumulated in the busi-
ness.[20]   Ingraham tells of a man who had amassed

[16]Mr. Gholson in Va. Leg.   Richmond Enquirer, Jan.
24, 1832.   Mr. Goode, ibid., Jan. 19. 1832.
[17](Ingraham) : The Southwest, Vol. 4, p. 234.
Vigne: Six Months in Am., p. 117.
Alexander: Transatlantic Sketches, p. 230.
[18]Liberator, Sept. 6, 1850.
[19]Mary Tremain: Slavery in D. C., p. 50.
[20]Abdy: Journal of a Residence and Tour in the U. S.,
Vol. II., p. 180.

more than a million dollars in this traffic.[21]   More instances might be given but this is enough to show that the traffic was profitable.

The cultivation of rice[22] and sugar, especially sugar, used up slaves rapidly. As a consequence slaves were in demand in the rice and sugar sections, not only because of the expansion of these industries, but to take the place of those that died. In 1829 the statement was made in a report of the Agricultural Society of Baton Rouge, Louisiana, that the annual loss of life on well conducted sugar plantations was two and one-half per cent. more than the annual increase. In 1830, the Hon. J. L. Johnson in a letter to the Secretary of the Treasury gave evidence of a thorough study of the subject and arrived at the same conclusion.[23]

We come now to consider the one thing, the prime factor, which brought about the wonderful agricultural prosperity of the Southwest—*cotton.* Sugar and rice could only be grown in certain

[21](Ingraham) : The Southwest. Vol. II., p. 245.
[22]Basil Hall : Travels in North America, 218-223.
[23]Stearns : Notes on Uncle Tom's Cabin, 174-5.

limited sections. Rice principally in South Carolina and sugar in Louisiana; but the cotton field
came to cover the larger part of nine great
States.

Until toward the end of the eighteenth century the production of cotton in this country was
very small. In 1793, however, Eli Whitney in-
vented his machine for separating the seed from
the cotton. This soon revolutionized the industry.
While the cotton crop of the United States in
1793 was only 5,000,000 pounds, by 1808 it had
increased to 80,000,000, and remained about the
same or rather declined during the war of 1812,
but the very year peace was established its production went up to 100,000,000 pounds, and the
year following (1816) to 125,000,000. By 1834
it had grown to 460,000,000.[24] During the whole
of this period, with slight fluctuations, cotton
continued high, but after 1835 it began to decline
and reached low-water mark at the average price
of 5¾ cents per pound in 1845, which was

---

[24]Woodbury's Report: 24th Cong., 1st Sess. Ex. Doc.
146, p. 7.

scarcely the cost of production.[25] However, the crop of 1839 according to the census reports was 790,479,275 pounds, nearly double the crop of the five years previous. During the next decade though the price went up after 1845[26] the crop increased less than 200,000,000 pounds being only 987,637,200 in 1849, but during the following ten years it more than doubled, being 2,397,238,-140 pounds in 1859.[27] Of this enormous crop the four States of Mississippi, Alabama, Louisiana and Georgia produced more than two-thirds, while Virginia contributed about 1-400.[28] But Virginia and North Carolina in 1801 had produced more than two-fifths of the cotton raised in the country. In 1826 when, according to the official reports they reached their greatest production, Virginia grew 25,000,000 pounds and North Carolina 18,000,000, or nearly five times as much as in 1801, yet this proportion had fallen to about one-seventh. Eight years afterward

---

[25]De Bow's Review: Vol. XXIII., p. 475.

[26]Hammond: Cotton Ind., Ap. 1.

[27]Census of 1890. Statistics of Agri., p. 42.

[28]Ibid.

Virginia's crop had fallen to 10,000,000 pounds
and North Carolina's to 9,500,000,[29] and their
production continued to decline.[30] Hammond
says that "the higher cost of raising cotton in the
more northern latitudes, and the uncertainty of
the plant reaching maturity before the arrival of
the frosts, prevented the rapid growth of cotton
culture in these States after 1830 which took
place elsewhere, especially as the continual decline
in the price of the staple only emphasized the dis-
advantages under which the planters of these
States labored."[31]

But while decline was noticeable in the Northern States, the States at the Southwest were going ahead by leaps and bounds. The same year
(1843) Alabama, Mississippi, and Louisiana,
from which no cotton had been reported in 1801,
produced together 232,000,000 pounds, while
South Carolina increased its crops from 2,000,000
to 65,500,000 and Georgia from 10,000,000 to
75,000,000 pounds during the same time.[32]

[29]Woodbury's Report, p. 13.
[30]Census, 1890. Statistics of Agri., p. 42.
[31]Hammond: The Cotton Industry, p. 49.
[32]Woodbury's Report, p. 13.

As the cotton field extended of course the demand for labor increased and that labor was necessarily negro slave labor, for it was thought that the white man could not endure work under a tropical sun, while the organism of the negro was especially adapted to it.[33] As a consequence negroes were secured from every possible source.

In short, negroes and cotton soon came to be inseparably associated. The amount of cotton that could be raised depended upon the number of negroes to be secured to work it. The value of a negro was measured by his usefulness in the cotton field.[34] De Bow estimated that in 1850 out of the 2,500,000 slaves in the Southern States about 1,800,000[35] of them, or nearly three-fourths were engaged in the cotton industry, leaving for all other purposes only about 700,000, or about the same number as there was in the whole United States in 1790, at which time the produc-

---

[33]Van Enrie: Negroes and Negro Slavery, p. 171.
  Parkinson: Tour in America, Vol. II., p. 421.

[34]Olmsted: Cotton Kingdom.   Vol. I., 15-16.   Ibid.:
Seaboard Slave States, p. 278.

[35]De Bow: Compendium, 7th Census, p. 94.

tion of cotton was only 1,500,000 pounds.[36]
Thus it is seen that while cotton demanded
all the increase of slaves from whatever
source from that time forward all other
things merely held their own. However,
if we subtract the number engaged in the sugar
industry, which was 150,000[37] in 1850 for the reason that it was a new crop developed during the
early part of the century,[38] it is noticed that other
things lost. From this we conclude it was only
natural that the surplus slave population of the
older slave States where it was useless was to
be drained off to the cotton States. Some of the
Southern papers, notably the "Richmond Enquirer," over and again called attention to the
relation of cotton and negroes. In 1859 it says:

"The price of cotton it is well known pretty
much regulates the price of slaves in the South,
and a bale of cotton and a 'likely nigger' are about
well balanced in the scale of pecuniary appreci-
ation."[39]

---

[36]Woodbury's Report, p. 7.
[37]De Bow: Compendium, 7th Census, p. 94.
[38]Ibid.: Industrial Resources, Vol. III., p. 275.
[39]Richmond Enquirer, July 29, 1859.

CHAPTER III.

THE AMOUNT AND EXTENT OF THE TRADE.

WE have already discussed the causes of the domestic slave trade. In this chapter it is our purpose, chiefly, to consider its amount and extent.

In this connection our first object will be to determine whether it was carried on as a business before 1808. It appears that there were exchanges of slaves going on among the States and territories before this time, but whether this was anything more than of an occasional or incidental nature is a question.

The statutes of some of the States give some light along this line. South Carolina in 1792 prohibited the introduction of slaves either by land or sea.[1] Delaware, however, as early as 1787, passed a law which recites that: "Sundry negroes and mulattoes, as well freeman as slaves,

---

[1] Acts Gen. Assembly of S. C. from Feb., 1791, to Dec., 1794, inclusive, Vol. I., 215.

have been exported and sold into other States, contrary to the principles of humanity and justice, and derogatory to the honor of this State."

This law prohibited their exportation without a permit.[2]   It seems to have been something more than merely incidental for it was amended in 1793, as follows:

"That from and after the first Tuesday of October next, the justice of the Court of General Quarter Sessions and Jail Delivery, or any two of them, shall have the like power to grant a licence or permit to export, sell or carry out for sale, any negro or mulatto slave from this State that five justices of the peace in open Sessions now have."[3]

We have evidence to show that, by 1802, Alexandria, in the District of Columbia, had become a sort of depot for the sale of slaves, and that men visited it from distant parts of the United States in order to purchase them.[4]

---

[2] Hurd: Law of Freedom and Bondage, Vol. II., p. 74-75.

[3] Laws of the State of Delaware, 1793, p. 105.

[4] Mr. Miner, of Pennsylvania, in a speech in Congress, January 6, 1829, read the following presentment made by the Grand Jury at Alexandria in 1802. "We the

About this time slaves were in great demand
and very high in Mississippi,[5] and probably, also,
in the new States of Kentucky and Tennessee.[6]
However, it is not to be supposed that the great
increase of the slave population in these sections
before 1815 was due, to any great extent, to the
domestic slave trade.   There were five causes
which may be assigned for this increase, of which
the domestic trade was, probably, among the least,
if not the least.   No doubt, the most important
was the immigration of slave holders with their
slaves.[7]   This immigration was considerable: the
white population of Tennessee and Kentucky
nearly trebled between 1790 and 1800, and between 1800 and 1810 it about doubled, and the

Grand Jury for the body of the County of Alexandria
in the District of Columbia, present as a grievance the
practice of persons coming from distant parts of the
United States into this district for the purpose of pur-
chasing slaves."—Gales and Seaton's Register of Debates in Congress, Vol. V., p. 177.   At this time the
foreign slave trade was prohibited by statutes in all the
states.

[5]Claibourne: Mississippi as a Province, Territory, and
State, Vol. I., p. 144.

[6]It is to be remembered that this was just before the
opening of the foreign slave trade by South Carolina.

[7]Monette: History of the Valley of the Mississippi,
Vol. II., pp. 177-191, 269, 195, 547.   Niles' Register,
Sept. 13 and Oct. 18, 1817.

population of Mississippi more than quadrupled
between 1800 and 1810.   Slaves, also, increased
in as great a ratio.[8]   Second, we consider the
South Carolina slave trade from 1804 to 1807
inclusive.   From a speech of Mr. Smith of South
were sold in the Carolinas, but that the most of
Carolina in the United States Senate, December
8, 1820, we learn that only a small part of the
negroes introduced in consequence of this trade
them were bought by the people of the Western
and Southwestern States and territories.[9]   Third,
was the natural increase.   Fourth would be the
illegal foreign slave trade,[10] and fifth is the domestic trade.   It is impossible to more than approximate the relative importance of these factors.

However, it seems very unlikely that the domestic trade was of much consequence before
1815.   Whatever impetus it may have received on
account of the demand for slaves just prior to

---

[8]Census 1870.   Population and Statistics, p. 4, 7 (re-
capitulation).

[9]Annals of Congress, 16th Congress, 2nd   Session,
p. 77.

[10]Above Chap. I.   Vincent Nolte, p. 189.   Am. Col.
So. Reports, Vol. I., p. 94.   Du Bois, p. 111.

the South Carolina trade, must have been checked
by the consequent heavy importation from abroad.
For, on account of this, slaves fell in price, as it
is said adults, at this time, generally sold in the
Southwest at one hundred dollars each.[11]

If the domestic slave trade had assumed any
importance, or even if it had been going on at all
before 1815, it seems more than likely that it
would have been remarked by travellers, many of
whom, both English and American, visited the
Southwest and other sections of the country during the period in question. But so far as we can
find, none of them make any mention of it whatever.[12] The newspapers of the time, also, are
silent in regard to the matter. Doubtless the
rise and development of the trade was hindered

[11]Clay's Col. Society Speech, Dec. 17, 1829.

[12]William Darby travelled all through the Southwestern part of the country from about 1805 to 1815,
and wrote two books: "A Geographical Description of
the State of Louisiana, Mississippi and the Territory of
Alabama, published in 1817, and the Emigrants' Guide,
1818. He visited both Natchez and New Orleans. F.
Cumming Sketches of a Tour to the Western Country,
1807 to 1809. John Bradbury: Travels in the Interior
of America in the years 1809-10-11, including a description of Upper Louisiana, together with the Illinois
and Western Territories. Christian Scutz: Travels on

or delayed by the War of 1812,[13] but almost immediately after the close of the war, it comes into notice and even prominence. In 1816 Paulding in his "Letters from the South" writes of it from personal observation, and also tells of a man who had even thus early made money in the business.[14]

At this time, indeed, conditions were very favorable to a growth of the domestic trade. The general prosperity and the high price of agricultural products, especially cotton and sugar,[15] caused a great demand for slave labor for the new and fertile lands of the South and Southwest. In 1817 and 1818 the buying up of negroes for these markets was fast becoming a regular business, and it was a very common thing to see gangs of them chained and marching toward the South.[16]

---

an Inland Voyage Through the States of New York, Pennsylvania, Virginia, Ohio, Kentucky, Tennessee, and through the territories of Indiana, Louisiana, Mississippi, and New Orleans in the years 1807, 1808. Vincent Nolte: Fifty Years in Both Hemispheres. And others.

[13]Niles' Reg., Vol. XIII., p. 119, Oct. 18, 1817.

[14](Paulding) : Letters from the South, pp. 122, 128.

[15]Hunt's Merchants' Magazine, Vol. VI., p. 473.

[16]Birkbeck: Notes on a Journey from the Coast of Virginia to the Territory of Illinois, p. 25. Palmer :

They were collected from various places by dealers and shipped down the Mississippi River in flat-boats. Fourteen of these loaded with slaves for sale were seen at Natchez at once about this time.[17]

The statement was made that 8,000 slaves were carried into Georgia in 1817 from the Northern slave holding States.[18] It would seem probable that the greater part of these may have been introduced by immigrants. However, the slave trade must have been great, for on December 20, 1817, the Georgia legislature passed a law to prohibit at once the importation of slaves for sale.[19]

Between 1810 and 1820 slaves in the four States of Georgia, Mississippi, Tennessee and Louisiana in round numbers increased from 202,-

Journal of Travels in the United States, p. 142. Francis Hall, Travels in Canada and the United States, p. 358.

[17]Fearon: Sketches of America, p. 268.

[18]Facts Respecting Slavery, p. 2 in (Yale) Slavery Pamphlet, Vol. LXI.

[19]Acts of the General Assembly of Georgia, p. 139. NOTE.—From 1810 to 1820 slaves increased in Georgia about 44,000, or 43 per cent. The illicit foreign traffic to this State was great during part of this time. Torrey says in 1817, that it was common for masters in Maryland, Delaware and District of Columbia to endeavor

ooo to 332,000,[20] and in some of the other States the increase was about as great. During the same time the white population in the States named increased from 419,000 to 645,000.[21] By far the greater part of this increase took place after 1815. To prove this we will take Louisiana as an example. In 1810 she had a population of 76,500,[22] and in 1815 near the close of the year her population, according to Monette, did not exceed 90,000,[23] an increase of only 12,000; but in 1820 it amounted to 154,000, of which more than 73,000 were negro slaves.[24] It appears that the slaves in Louisiana increased only about 2,000 or 2,500 from 1810 to 1815, but between 1815 and 1820 there was an increase of about 37,000.[25] This wonderful increase in population in the West and Southwest is to be accounted for by the

to reform bad slaves by threatening to sell them to Georgia. Torrey: Portraiture of Slavery in United States, p. 37.

[20]Census 1870, Vol. Pop. and Statistics, p. 7.

[21]Ibid., p. 4.

[22]Ibid., pp. 4, 6, 7.

[23]Monette: History of Mississippi Valley, Vol. II., p. 515.

[24]Census 1870. Pop. and Social Statistics, pp. 4, 6, 7.

[25]In 1810 there were in Louisiana 34,660 slaves and 7,585 free colored (census reports); according to Mo-

fact that after the close of the War of 1812 immigration again set in these directions, and, as most
of the immigrants without doubt were from the
older Southern States, they carried with them
the slaves which they had in their native States.[26]
Another source from which this region received
slaves at this time was through the operation of
the illicit foreign trade. It is probable that 10,000
or 15,000 a year were thus introduced.[27] It therefore seems that up to this time to the domestic
trade is due probably only a minor part of the
increase of the slave population of this section.

During the twenties, however, if we are to
give credit to the statements of travellers, the
trade reached very great proportions. Baltimore,
Norfolk, Richmond, Washington and other places
had already become centres. Agents were placed

nette (Vol. II., p. 515) in 1815 there were about 45,000
blacks. It is reasonable to suppose that at least 8,500 of
these must have been free negroes as there were 10,476
free negroes in Louisiana in 1820. (Census reports.)
    [26]Monette: Vol. IV., pp. 281, 433, 444, 445. Evans:
A Pedestrious Tour, p. 173. Niles' Reg., Vol. XIII.,
pp. 40, 110. Sept. 13, Oct. 18, 1817.
    [27]State Papers, 16th Congress, 1st Session, Vol. III.,
Doc. 42. Niles' Reg., May 2, 1818, Jan. 22, 1820; Sept.
6, 1817. Wm. Jay: Miscellaneous Writings, p. 277,
Chap. I. above.

in these cities to attend to purchase and shipment. "And thousands and tens of thousands," such is the language of an English tourist, were purchased in Virginia and Maryland for sale in Georgia, Louisiana and other States.[28] Blane, another Englishman, who visited the United States about the same time, is more to the point.

"It is computed," he says, "that every year from ten to fifteen thousand slaves are sold from the States of Delaware, Maryland and Virginia and sent to the South."[29]

Basil Hall was informed, in 1827 or 1828, that during certain seasons of the year, "all the roads, steamboats and packets are crowded with troops of negroes on their way to the slave markets of the South.[30] Vessels, indeed, from the selling States were sometimes seen in New Orleans with as many as two hundred negroes aboard.[31]

This transportation of negroes from the border

---

[28](Isaac Candler): A Summary View of America during a Journey in 1822-23; p. 273.

[29](Wm. Newnham Blane): An Excursion through the United States and Canada, p. 226.

[30]Basil Hall: Travels in North America, Vol. II., p. 219.

[31]Ibid.: p. 220. Niles' Reg., Dec. 27, 1828.

States to the South and Southwest from about
1826 to 1832 may be partly accounted for by the
probable falling off in the illicit importations[32]
and by the fact that cotton and tobacco, which
were the staples of some of the border States,
were comparatively low in price,[33] making them
very unprofitable crops to cultivate in these States.
The cotton raised in North Carolina and Virginia
decreased almost half during this time.[34]   While
it appears as if the lower price of cotton merely
had the effect in the new States to increase the
acreage in order to make up for the deficiency
in price.   In the new States there was a wonderful increase in production during this period.[35]
Slaves, therefore, were of much less productive
value in the border States, while in the new States
the demand for them was scarcely lessened.

The "New Orleans Mercantile Advertiser," of
January 21, 1830, says:

"Arrivals by sea and river, within a few days,
have added fearfully to the number of slaves

---

[32]Du Bois, p. 128.
[33]Hunt's Merchants' Magazine, Vol. VI., p. 473.
[34]Woodbury's Report, p. 13.
[35]Ibid.

brought to this market for sale. New Orleans is the complete mart for the slave trade—and the Mississippi is becoming a common highway for the traffic.[36]

In the summer of 1831, New Orleans imported 371 negroes in one week, nearly all of whom were from Virginia.[37]

In the same year, August 1831, an insurrection of slaves, in which a number of white people were murdered, occurred in Southampton County, Virginia.[38] This caused much excitement throughout the slave States. It opened the eyes of the people to the danger of a large slave population. It seemed, for a while, that it would have a very detrimental effect upon the domestic slave trade, for several importing States began to consider the advisability of prohibiting the further introduction of slaves. Two of the largest importing States,[39] indeed, passed such laws: Louisiana, which, in March, 1831, had repealed her law

---

[36]Quoted from the African Repository, Vol. V., p. 381.
[37]Niles' Reg., Nov. 26, 1831.
[38]Richmond Enquirer, Aug. 30, 1831.
[39]Dew: Debates in Virginia Legislature, p. 59. In (Yale) Slav. Pamp., Vol. XLVII.

regulating the importation of slaves[40] in November of the same year, at an extra session of her legislature enacted a law against their importation for sale.[41] And, in January, 1832, Alabama followed suit.[42]

The Virginia Legislature of 1831-2, also took up the question of slavery and with open doors vigorously discussed methods of emancipation, and of getting rid of the negro population. It was recognized that the value of slaves in Virginia depended greatly upon the Southern and Western markets. It was feared that other buying States would follow the lead of Louisiana, thus cutting off the outlet of Virginia's surplus slaves, and while the whites were constantly emigrating, the rapidly increasing black population would tend to become congested in the State, producing a condition of society alarming to contemplate.[43]

But these forebodings were far from ever being realized. Indeed, even before the end of

---

[40]Acts Legislature Louisiana, 1831, p. 78.
[41]Acts of Extra Sess. of 10th Leg. of Louisiana, p. 4.
[42]Laws of Alabama, 1831-2, p. 12.
[43]Slavery Speeches in Virginia Legislature, Richmond Enquirer, Jan. 19, 21, 24; March 30, 1832.

the year the conjunction of two causes produced
a great demand for slaves and they were soon
higher in price than they had been for years.
First, planters from the cotton-growing States
visited Virginia in great numbers in order to
make purchases of slaves, doubtless, thinking
they could buy cheaply, as it seemed that on account of the Southampton Insurrection Virginia
was determined to get rid of her slaves at all
hazards.[44] Second, the most important was the
advance in price of cotton. This began, also,
in 1832. It continued to rise for several years
and by 1836 it had doubled in price,[45] while by
1839 its production, also, had nearly doubled.
This increase was due almost wholly to the South
and Southwest, Mississippi alone producing
nearly one-fourth of the entire crop.[46]

As a consequence we should expect to note a
corresponding briskness in the slave trade. Such,
indeed, was the case. We have no reason to think
that more slaves were ever exported to the South

[44]Dew: Debate in Virginia Legislature, p. 50.
(Yale) Slav. Pamp., Vol. XLVII.
[45]Hunt's Merchants' Magazine, Vol. VI., p. 473.
[46]Census 1890, Statistics of Agriculture, p. 42.

from the Northern slave States during any equal period of time than there were from 1832 to 1836 inclusive. Of these 1836 is easily the banner year.

In 1832 it was estimated by Prof. Dew that Virginia annually exported for sale to other States 6,000 slaves.[47] During the thirties, or even before the slave trade was carried on between the selling and buying States with about the same regularity as the exchanges of cotton, flour, sugar and rice.[48] Vessels engaged in the business advertised their accommodations. One trader, John Armfield, had three which were scheduled to leave Alexandria for New Orleans, alternately, the first and fifteenth of each month during the shipping season.[49]

That the trade had become extensive is evidenced by the newspapers. Up to 1820 it was very uncommon to find a trader's advertisement

[47]Dew: Debates in Virginia Legislature, p. 49. (Yale) Sl. Pamp., Vol. XLVII. Dew made this statement in a paper in which his argument required him to prove that the greatest possible number were sent from Virginia.

[48]Liberator, May 18, 1833.

[49]Daily National Intelligencer, Feb. 10, 1836.

in a newspaper, but even before 1830 such advertisements had become very plentiful. One could
hardly pick up a paper published in the selling
States, especially those of the Eastern Shore of
Maryland and Eastern Virginia, without finding
one or more. These advertisements often continued from month to month and from year to
year.[50]

An example or two may be interesting:

"Cash for Negroes:—I wish to purchase 600
or 700 negroes for the New Orleans market, and
will give more than any purchaser that is now or
hereafter may come into the market." Richard
C. Woolfolk.[51]

"Cash for Negroes:—We will give cash for
200 negroes between the ages of 15 and 25 years
old of both sexes. Those having that kind of
property for sale will find it to their interest to
give us a call." Finnall and Freeman.[52]

[50]Snow Hill (Md.) Messenger and Worcester Co.
Advertiser, May 14, 1832, Feb. 11, 1833, March 11,
1833. Winyaw Intelligencer (S. C.), Dec. 11, 1803.
Norfolk and Portsmouth Herald, Jan. 16, 1826. Cambridge Chronicle (Md.), Feb. 12, 1831. Charleston (S.
C.), Mercury, Feb. 18, 1833.
[51]Village Herald (Princess Anne, Md.), Jan. 7, 1831.
[52]The Virginia Herald (Fredericksburg, Va.), Jan. 2.
1836.

The number of slaves currently estimated to have been transported to the South and Southwest during 1835 and 1836 almost staggers belief.   The "Maryville (Tenn.) Intelligencer" made the statement in 1836 that in 1835 60,000 sslaves passed through a Western town on their way to the Southern market.[53] Also, in 1836, the "Virginia (Wheeling) Times" says, intelligent men estimated the number of slaves exported from Virginia during the preceding twelve months as 120,000 of whom about two-thirds were carried there by their masters, leaving 40,-000 to have been sold.[54] The Quarterly Anti-Slavery Magazine," July 1837, gives the "Natchez Courier" as authority for the estimate that during 1836, 250,000 slaves were transported to Alabama, Mississippi, Louisiana and Arkansas from the older slave States.[55] A committee, in 1837, appointed by the citizens of Mobile to enquire into the cause of the prevalent financial stringency stated in their report that for the preceding four

[53]Slavery and the Internal Slave Trade, p. 17.
[54]Ibid., p. 13.
[55]Quarterly Anti-Slavery Magazine, Vol. II., p. 411.

years Alabama had annually purchased from other States $10,000,000 worth of slave property.[56]

When the panic of 1837 came upon Mississippi, it was thought, it seems, to have been caused through the amount of money sent out of the State in the purchase of slaves, and Governor Lynch, upon the petition of the people, convened the legislature in extra session, and in his message to it says:

"The question which presents itself and which I submit for your deliberation [is]—whether the passage of an act prohibiting the introduction of slaves into this State as merchandise may not have a salutary effect in checking the drain of capital annually made upon us by the sale of this description of property."[57]

The panic of 1837 caused a falling off in the domestic slave trade, and the low price of cotton which continued until 1846[58] hindered its revival. The falling off in the trade is shown by the fact

[56]Sl. and Internal Sl. Trade, p. 14. Christian Freeman, July 24, 1845.

[57]The Mississippian, April 21, 1837.

[58]Hammond: The Cotton Industry, Appendix I. De Bow's Review, Vol. XXIII., p. 475.

that the per cent. of increase in the slave population of the cotton States was scarcely half as
great between 1840 and 1850 as during the previous decade.[59]   The slave trade, however, seems
to have become brisker in 1843, for while only
2,000 slaves are said to have been sold in Washington in 1842, in 1843, 5,000 were sold there.[60]
It does not necessarily follow, however, that all
these were sent South.   The increased number
of sales was caused by two things: the decline
in the price of tobacco,[61] and the renewed activity
in the sugar industry incident upon a new duty
on sugar.[62]   This gave rise to a demand for slave
labor upon the sugar plantations of the South,
but it was a very limited demand.   During this
period the decline in the value of slaves was great
in some States,[63] and it appears very probable
there was a general depreciation in value.   However, before 1850 three important things had
happened, each of which had an effect upon the

[59]De Bow's Review, Vol. XXIII., p. 477.
[60]Emancipator, Oct. 26, and Nov. 26, 1843.
[61]De Bow: Industrial Resources, Vol. III., p. 349.
[62]Ibid.: p. 275.   Emancipator, Oct. 26, 1843.
[63]Liberator, May 19, 1837, May 24, 31, 1839, April 30,
1847.

slave trade. First, the admission of Texas, December, 1845; second, the gradual increase in the price of cotton after 1845; third, the discovery of gold in California. The first opened a large cotton country to development and the required slave labor could be legally supplied only from the United States. The rise in cotton which continued almost uniformly until 1860[64] caused a new impetus to be given to its culture, and the discovery of gold in California infused new life into all the channels of trade.

In a few years, indeed, after 1845, the demand for slaves seems to have been greater than the supply. A writer in the "Richmond Examiner," in 1849, says:

"It being a well ascertained fact that Virginia and Maryland will not be able to supply the great demand for negroes which will be wanted in the South this fall and next spring, we would advise all who are compelled to dispose of them in this market to defer selling until the sales of the present crop of cotton can be realized as the price then must be very high owing to two reasons:

[64]Hammond: Cotton Industry, Appendix I.

First, the ravages of the cholera, and secondly, the high price of cotton."[65]

Indeed, during the fifteen years prior to 1860 the demand for slaves became so great that it caused an increase of one hundred per cent. in their price.[66]   However, there was not a great increase in the domestic slave trade.   According to a custom house report there were shipped from Baltimore in a little less than two years, in 1851 and 1852 only 1,033 negroes.[67]   This is certainly not a large showing though it is probable a great many were sent overland to the South from this place during the same time.

In a speech before the Southern Convention at Savannah in 1856, Mr. Scott, of Virginia, made the statement that not more than half the lands in the sugar and cotton-growing States had been reduced to cultivation, and that all the valuable slaves in Virginia, Maryland, Kentucky and Missouri would be required to develop them.[68]   But at this time the prosperity of the latter militated

---

[65]Quoted from the National Era, Sept. 27, 1849.
[66]De Bow's Review, Vol. XXVI., p. 649.
[67]Key to Uncle Tom's Cabin, p. 149.
[68]De Bow's Review, Vol. XXII., pp. 216-218.

against the transfer of labor to the cotton-growing States. Probably the conditions in the border States is best described by quoting from a writer in "De Bow's Review" in 1857:

"The difficulty," he says, "of procuring slaves at reasonable rates, has already been severely felt by the cotton planters, and this difficulty is constantly increasing. The production of rice, tobacco, wheat, Indian corn, etc., with stock raising, in those States affords nearly as profitable employment for slave labor as cotton planting in other States. They have not, as is generally supposed, a redundancy of slave labor, nor are they likely to have so long as their present prosperity continues.

"The recent full development of the rich agricultural and mineral resources of these States, indeed, by an immense demand for their staple productions, have not only given profitable employment to slave labor, but has improved the pecuniary condition of the slave owner and placed him above the necessity of parting with his slave property."[69]

[69]P. A. Morse, of Louisiana. De Bow's Review, Vol. XXIII., p. 480. Note.—The statement was made by a

Even Olmsted, inadvertedly, no doubt, gives evidence of the prosperity of Virginia, a little before this time, when he says that in the tobacco factories of Richmond and Petersburg slaves were in great demand and received a hundred and fifty to two hundred dollars and expenses a year.[70] In North Carolina, also, good hands would bring about the same wages.[71]

Though the labor market in the border States was greater than the natural increase of the negro, yet it was hardly to be compared to the Southern demand. As a consequence, when debt, or necessity, or other reason, compelled the sale of slaves, they were often bought by traders and exported.[72] The statement was made by Mr. Jones, of Georgia, in the Savannah Convention, 1856, that negroes were even then worth from $1,000 to $1,500 each, and that there were ten purchasers to one seller.[73]

South Carolina delegate to the Southern Convention at Montgomery in 1858, that Virginia was then the best market in the Union for the slaves of his State. De Bow's Review. Vol. XXIV., p. 595.

[70]Olmsted: Seaboard Slave States, p. 127.

[71]Liberator, Jan. 12, 1855.

[72]De Bow's Review, Vol. XXVI. p. 650.

[73]Ibid.: Vol. XXII., p. 222.

Indeed, so great was the demand for slaves at this time that the advisability of reopening the African slave trade became one of the principal topics of discussion in Southern Agricultural and Commercial Conventions.[74] In fact, the Vicksburg Convention, 1859, passed a resolution in favor of reopening the African trade.[75]

The New Orleans newspapers during all this period give evidence of the domestic trade. It was very common during the shipping season to see advertisements to the effect that the subscriber, a negro trader, had received, or had just arrived from Virginia, Maryland, the Carolinas or elsewhere, with a large lot of negroes which were offered for sale. Usually the number would be given as fifty, seventy-five, or even a hundred. This would be qualified by the statement that they would be constantly receiving fresh lots. The same advertisement would continue in the same paper for months and even years. Sometimes half a dozen of these could be found in a single

---

[74] De Bow's Review, Vol. XVIII., p. 628; Vol. XXII., pp. 216, 217, 218; Vol. XXIV., pp. 581, 585, 574, 588.
[75] Ibid.: Vol. XXVII., p. 470.

issue of a paper. It would be impossible even to
approximate from this source the number sold
during any given time, for it is likely the number
offered for sale bore but little relation to the
actual number sold.   The States of Maryland,
Virginia and the Carolinas were most conspicuous
in these advertisements.[76]

Writers on the subject seem to be pretty well
agreed that during this period, or during the fifties, about 25,000 slaves were annually sold
South from the Northern slave States.[77]

It is interesting to notice in this connection
what the Census Reports have to show. But in
reading it should be remembered that no account
is taken of the sale of slaves except as they took
place between the buying and selling States. So
the sale of slaves between Virginia and Maryland

---

[76]New Orleans Picaynne, Jan. 8, 15, 1846; Feb. 3,
Dec. 10, 1856; Jan. 7, 14, 1858; Dec. 31, 1859.

[77]Sumner's Works, Vol. V., p. 62; Olmsted, Cotton
Kingdom, Vol. I., (note) p. 58. Chambers: Slavery
and Color, p. 148. Chase and Sanborn: The North and
the South, p. 22.
    NOTE.—The estimate of 60,000 given in Hunt's Mer-
chants' Magazine is scarcely worth consideration.
Hunt's Magazine, Vol. XLIII., p. 642.

are not indicated nor those between Mississippi
and Alabama.

The slave population of Alabama, Arkansas,
Georgia, Louisiana, Mississippi, South Carolina,
Tennessee and Missouri in 1820 was in round
numbers 644,000, in 1830 997,000 being an increase of 353,000. The slave population in the
selling States of Virginia, Maryland, Delaware,
North Carolina, Kentucky and the District of
Columbia at the same periods[78] was 873,000 and
993,000 respectively, being an increase in these
States of 120,000. Total increase of slaves in
both sections during the decade, 473,000, from
which we deduct 50,000 due to the illicit foreign
traffic,[79] leaving 423,000 from natural increase
or about 28 per cent. Had the selling States increased at this ratio, instead of 120,000 their increase would have been 244,000. This would
seem to indicate that at least 12,400 annually
were carried South during this decade. However, only the smaller part of these, and those of
the following decade as well, were transported

---

[79]See Chap. I., this volume.
[78]Census 1820 and 1830.

through the operation of the domestic slave trade.
Mr. P. A. Morse, of Louisiana, writing in 1857,
says that the augmentation of slaves within the
cotton States was caused mostly by the migration
of slave owners.[80]   The "Virginia Times," in
1836, says of the number of slaves exported during the preceding twelve months "not more than
one-third have been sold, the others having been
carried by their owners who have removed.[81] We
conclude from these and other sources[82] that at
least three-fifths of the removals of slaves from
the border slave States to those farther South
from 1820 to 1850 were due to emigration.[83]

[80]De Bow's Review, Vol. XXIII., p. 476.

[81]Slavery and the Internal Slave Trade, p. 13.

[82]Andrews: Sl. and Domestic Sl. Trade, pp. 174. 171,
117, 167.   Smedes: Memorials of a Southern Planter.
pp. 48-50.   Cary: Slave Trade, Domestic and Foreign,
p. 109.   (Ingraham): The Southwest, Vol. II., p. 233.
We have not taken into account the slaves brought
by planters themselves independently of the traders.
See Dew's "Debates," Pro-Slavery Argument, p. 361.

[83]Other things which perhaps ought to be considered,
but which do not seem to modify results are mentioned
in this note; i.e., the mortality on the sugar plantations
(Stearns' Notes on Uncle Tom's Cabin, pp. 174-5). and
the deaths caused by removal of slaves from a northern climate (Olmsted: Journey in the Back Country,
122; Chambers: Slavery and Color, 147-8).   Negroes
advertised for sale in the far South were often adver-

Thus it is shown that probably 5,000[84] slaves were annually exported by the selling States from 1820 to 1830 by means of the domestic trade.

In the next decade adding Florida to the buy-

---

tised as acclimated (Mississippi Republican, Sept. 17, 1823; Daily Picayune, Jan. 30, 1856). To offset the loss of life thus caused it is well to remember that the increase of slaves carried to the South was not taken into account, but treated as if they too were carried there. For instance, 1,000 slaves imported in 1830 would at a 20 per cent. rate of increase number 1,200 by 1840, or to take the middle date 1835, 1,100. So each 1,000 slaves brought in during the decade would increase by 100. If 40,000 were introduced by the illicit foreign traffic between 1830 and 1840, and 106,000 by the trade from the border States, it would mean a natural increase of 14,600 for the ten years. This it seems would offset both the deaths on the sugar plantation, and those caused by removal to another climate.

Next to be considered are refugees and manumitted slaves; Miss Martineau said that there were about 10,000 negroes in Upper Canada about 1838, chiefly fugitive slaves (W. Travel., Vol. II., p. 101). The Census of 1860 reports that (Vol. Pop. XVI.) 1,011 slaves escaped in 1850, and only 803 in 1860, and that the slave population increased in slave states more than 20 per cent. during the 10 years, and free colored population in the free States only about 13 per cent. It is estimated in De Bow's Industrial Resources (Vol. III., p. 129) that about 1,540 annually escaped. (For other estimates see Seibert Underground R.R., pp. 192, 221 et seq.)

The Census of 1860 reports that more than 3,000

---

[84]This about accords with Alexander, who said that by means of the internal trade about 4,000 or 5,000 arrived in the Southern States annually. Transatlantic Sketches, p. 230.

ing State and transferring South Carolina[85] and
Missouri[86] to the selling list, we find that in 1830
and in 1840 the buying States had 672,000 and
1,127,000 respectively, being an increase of 455,-
000; while for the same periods the selling
States had 1,333,000 and 1,361,000, being an in-

---

were manumitted in census year of 1860, but this was
more than twice as many as in 1850. (1860 Vol. Pop.,
p. XV.). To offset the fugitive slaves and those manumitted the following is given: kidnapped free negroes
from a few hundred to two or three thousand yearly
(below, p.   ); free negroes sold into slavery for jail
fees, etc. (Liberator, Nov. 19. 1841, July 17. 1834;
Speech of Mr. Miner in Congress Jan. 7, 1829; (Sturge:
A Visit to the U. S., p. 101) voluntary return to slavery
—many States made laws before 1860 to provide for
such action on the part of the slaves. (Hurd, Vol.
II., p. 12, 24, 94, et seq.).

The things as mentioned above do not modify the
amount of the domestic slave trade as indicated by the
statistical review in the text. If one should argue that
the allowances we have made are not sufficient, we
would ask him to take notice also that it is more than
probable that most of the manumissions and escapes
from slavery were in the border States, and to that
extent lessens the amount of the apparent slave trade.
It is impossible to be definite here, we can only approximate.

---

[85]Between 1830 and 1840 the number of increase in
South Carolina was only about 12,000, while during the
previous decade it was about 57,000, if for no other
reason showing her to be an exporting State.

[86]Shaffner: The War in America, p. 256. (Ingraham): The Southwest, Vol. II., p. 237. It was rather
hard to determine whether Missouri should be classed

crease of 28,000. The whole increase, therefore, was 483,000,[87] deducting 40,000 due to illicit foreign trade,[88] we have 443,000 or about 22 per cent. as the natural increase. Had the selling States increased at same rate it would have been 293,-000 for the decade. Deducting 28,000 we find that 265,000 can be accounted for only as having been exported. Deducting three-fifths for emigration we have, removing 106,000 for the domestic traffic, an average of 10,600 per year.

By 1850, the buying States had another increase of 478,000 and the selling States 180,000. Total increase from 1840 to 1850, 658,000.[89] Deducting 50,000 illicitly imported,[90] we have 606,-000 or about 24 per cent. total increase. Accordingly the selling States should have a natural increase of 326,000. Deducting the actual number

---

with selling or buying States. It is likely she did some of both as did some others. But practically all her increase after 1830 at least (aside from natural increase) seemed to be due to immigration from Kentucky and Virginia, though her increase was very large, we think she would rank as a selling State anyhow after 1830.

[87]Census 1830 and 1840.
[88]Chap. I., this volume.
[89]Census 1840 and 1850.
[90]Chap. I., this volume.

we have left 146,000, which must have been transported. Deducting three-fifths on account of emigration, there would remain about 58,000 or nearly 6,000 per year for the domestic trade.

Adding Texas to the buying States in 1850, they then have 1,663,000, and in 1860 2,296,-000, or an increase of 633,000 during the decade.   And the selling States 1,541,000 and 1,657,000 respectively, being an increase of 116,-000.   Total increase 749,000.[91]   Deducting 70,000 which were brought in by illicit trade[92] we have a remainder of 679,000 or 21 per cent. natural increase.   From natural increase selling States should have had 207,000 more than the actual. Deducting three-fifths on account of emigration leaves a little more than 8,000 per year sold South annually for these ten years.

It is very probable that the emigration to the cotton States fell off during the fifties owing to the great prosperity in the border States, and it might be fair to reduce the number estimated to have been carried South by emigration to one-

[91]Census 1850 and 1860.
[92]Chap. I., this volume.

third or one-half, which would leave ten or twelve thousand per year for the domestic slave trade.

We feel quite confident that this statistical review of the domestic slave trade, based as it is upon the Census Reports, gives a truer idea of the actual amount of the trade between the selling and the buying States than could be got from any other sources.

CHAPTER IV

WERE SOME STATES ENGAGED IN BREEDING AND RAISING NEGROES FOR SALE?

As we now have a somewhat definite idea as to the amount of the domestic slave trade the next questions which naturally claim our attention are: Were some States consciously and purposely engaged in breeding and raising negroes for the Southern market, and also, what were the sources of supply for the trade? The former of these queries is, no doubt, the most controverted and difficult part of our subject.

The testimony of travellers and common opinion generally seems to have been in the affirmative. A quotation or two will suffice to show the trend: The Duke of Saxe Weimar says, "Many owners of slaves in the States of Maryland and Virginia have . . . nurseries for slaves whence the planters of Louisiana, Mississippi and other Southern States draw their supplies."[1]

In a "Narrative of a Visit to the American Churches," the writer, in speaking of the accumulation of negroes in the Gulf States, says: "Slaves are generally bred in some States as cattle for the Southern market."[2] And the Rev. Philo Tower, writing about twenty years later draws a more vivid picture. "Not only in Virginia," he says, "but also in Maryland, North Carolina, Kentucky, Tennessee and Missouri, as much attention is paid to the breeding and growth of negroes as to that of horses and mules. . . . It is a common thing for planters to command their girls and women (married or not) to have children; and I am told a great many negro girls are sold off, simply and mainly because they did not have children."[3]

[1]Bernard, Duke of Saxe Weimar, Travels Through North America, 1825-26, Vol. II., p. 63.

[2]Reed and Matheson: Visit to the Am. Churches, Vol. II., p. 173.

[3]Tower: Slavery Unmasked, p. 53. NOTE.—"The following story was told me by one conversant with the facts as they occurred on Mr. J.'s plantation, containing about 100 slaves. One day the owner ordered all the women into the barn; he followed them whip in hand, and told them he meant to flog them all to death; they, as a matter of course, began to cry out, 'What

Undoubtedly some planters in all the slave States resorted to questionable means of increasing their slave stock, but that it was a general custom to multiply negroes in order to have them to sell is very improbable.

Many of these travellers show prejudice. We have wondered, therefore, whether it were too much to assume that they had more thought for the effect their narrative would produce in the North or in England than for its truth. Is it not probable that foreigners may have got their information about breeding slaves when in the free States rather than actual evidence of such an industry where the industry was supposed to be carried on? It seems, at any rate, more than

---

have I done, Massa?' 'What have I done, Massa?' He replied: 'Damn you, I will let you know what you have done; you don't breed. I have not had a young one from you for several months.' They promptly told him they could not breed while they had to work in the rice ditches."

Slavery Unmasked was published in 1856. Exactly the same story as above, almost verbatim, is found in "Interesting Memoirs and Documents Relating to American Slavery," published in 1846. The fact that this story is told in different books published ten years apart indicates that such instances were very rare. It seemed strange that each writer should claim to have received the story from a friend, or "one conversant

probable that the exceptional cases which they found were made to appear as the general rule. Then, too, the very fact that some States sold great numbers of slaves was sufficient evidence to some, no doubt, that they were engaged in the business of raising them for sale. It seems very natural that this should be inferred.   Consequently travellers reported that certain sections were engaged in breeding and raising slaves for market.   They made the accusation that the so-called "breeding States" were in the slave-breeding business for profit.   But was it profitable? If not, why were they in this business?

A negro above eighteen years of age would bring on an average about $300 in the selling States from 1815 to, say, 1845.   Sometimes he would bring a little more, sometimes less.[4]   Be-

with the facts," for one seems to have copied directly from the other.   It was no doubt mere hearsay with both writers.

Others on slave breeding are: Buckingham: Slave States of America, Vol. I., p. 182; Miss Martineau: Society in America, Vol. II., p. 41.   Jay; Miscellaneous Writings, p. 457.   Abdy: Journal of a Residence in the United States, Vol. II., p. 90.   Rankin: Letters on American Slavery, p. 35.   Candler: A Summary View of America, p. 277.   Kemble: Journal of a Residence on a Georgian Plantation, pp. 60, 122.

tween the age of ten and the time of sale we will
suppose the slave paid for his keeping. But before that time he would be too small to work.
There was always some defective stock which
could not be sold;[5] this, taken in connection with
the fact that all negroes did not live to be ten
years of age, probably not more than half,[6] we
shall be under the necessity of deducting about
one-half of the $300 on this account. This will
leave $150 or $15 per year for the possible ex-
pense of raising him. A bushel of corn a month
would have been about $8 per year for corn;
fifty pounds for meat $4. It is not likely he could
have been clothed for less than $3, and the $15 is
gone, with nothing left for incidentals. We think
the above a very fair estimate. In 1829 the aver-

---

[4]Proceedings and Debates of the Virginia State Constitutional Convention, 1829-30, p. 178. Dew: Debates
in Virginia Legislature, 1831-2. Pro-Slavery Argument, p. 358. Andrews: Domestic Slave Trade, p. 77.

[5]Chambers: Am. Slavery and C. Laws, p. 148.

[6]Kemble: Journal of a Residence on a Georgia Plantation, pp. 190, 191, 199, 204, 214, 215. We get from
these that out of about 74 born 42 died very young.

[7]Stuart: Three Years in North America, Vol. II.,
p. 103. He says it cost $35 per year to feed and clothe
an adult negro a year. Must cost half that much for a
young one.

age price of negroes in Virginia was estimated at only $150 each.[8]

Why did not the border slave States raise hogs instead of negroes? Bacon was at a good price during that period.[9]

The fact is the negroes probably increased without any consideration for their master's wishes in the matter. A planter could stop raising hogs whenever he might choose, but it seemed to be hardly within the province of the master to limit the increase of his negroes. And the better they were treated evidently the faster the increase. A man who had one or two hundred negroes, and had scruples about selling them, unless he should be able to add to his landed estate as they increased was in a bad predicament. It seems some such men had the welfare of their negroes at heart and used every means to keep them. Andrews tells of one:

"A gentleman," he says, "in one of the poorer counties of Virginia has nearly 200 slaves whom he employs upon a second rate plantation of

---

[8]Proceedings and Debates of Virginia State Con. Convention, 1829-30, p. 178.
[9]Hunt's Merchants' Magazine, Vol. VI., p. 473.

8,000 or 10,000 acres, and who constantly brought him into debt, at length he found it necessary to purchase a smaller plantation of good land in another county which he continues to cultivate for no other purpose than to support his negroes.[10]

Sometimes men who were in prosperous circumstances would buy land as fast as their slaves increased and settle them upon it.[11]

Slaves were seldom sold until they were over ten years of age,[12] consequently if it were true that the border States made a business of breeding and raising them for sale we should naturally expect to find in these States a much greater proportion under ten than in the buying States. To determine the truth of this we shall have recourse to the Census Reports. The States of Virginia, Maryland, Kentucky and North Carolina, in 1830, had, in round numbers 984,000 slaves, of which 349,000 were under ten years of age, and 635,000 over. This shows that in these

---

[10]Andrews: Slavery and the Domestic Slave Trade, p. 110.
[11]Chambers: Am. Slavery and Color, p. 194.
[12]Ibid., p. 148.

States there were 182 over ten years of age to
every 100 under ten.   Taking an equal number
of the principal cotton-growing and slave-buying
States, say, Georgia, Mississippi, Alabama and
Tennessee, we find that they had 346,000 over ten
and 196,000 under ten,[13] consequently for every
176 of the former they had 100 of the latter.
Therefore, at this time, the principal so-called
"slave-breeding" States had a smaller number of
slaves under ten years than an equal number of
buying States.   The numbers, it will be seen,
differ as the ratios 100-182 and 100-176.

In 1840 there were in the Southern States about
2,486,000 slaves, of whom about 844,000 were
under ten years of age, on an average, therefore,
of 100 under ten to every 194 over.   Taking each
State separately we find that Virginia had just
an average, having 100 of the former to 194 of the
latter; Maryland, 100 to every 203; Delaware,
100 to 218;   District of Columbia, 100 to 280;
Kentucky, 100 to 179; North Carolina, 100 to
176; Missouri, 100 to 172; South Carolina, 100
to 205; Louisiana, 100 to 267; Mississippi, 100

---

[13]Census of 1830.

to 206; Florida, 100 to 220; Georgia, 100 to
188; Arkansas, 100 to 195; Tennessee, 100 to
170 and Alabama, 100 to 190.[14] Thus it is shown
that the buying States of Alabama, Georgia and
Tennessee each had more children in proportion
to their slave population than Virginia; and that
Maryland and Delaware had about the same
proportion as the buying States of Mississippi,
Florida and Arkansas. It would hardly be fair,
however, to compare the District of Columbia
with Louisiana.

In 1860 we find that the proportion of slave
children under ten years of age is much less in
all the States than in 1840.[15] In Virginia, at this
time, there were 100 under ten years to 227 over
that age; Delaware 100 to 233; Maryland, 100
to 229; Kentucky, 100 to 204; South Carolina,
100 to 224; North Carolina, 100 to 202;
Missouri, 100 to 190; Georgia, 100 to 221;
Louisiana, 100 to 285; Mississippi, 100 to
242; Texas, 100 to 209; Arkansas, 100 to 219;

---

[14]Census of 1840.

[15]We do not know why unless it is because slaves
being higher more care was taken of them, which as
a consequence caused them to live longer.

Tennessee, 100 to 200; Alabama, 100 to 221 and Florida 100 to 224.[16] This schedule shows that the buying States which had a greater number of slave children in proportion to their slave population in 1860, than Virginia, Maryland and Delaware, were Georgia, Arkansas, Tennessee, Alabama, Texas, and Florida.

It is noticeable in both schedules that the State of Louisiana is an exception. The proportion of children there was much less than in the other States. This is probably due to the strenuous work on sugar plantations. It is also noticeable that the Western States had the greatest proportional number of children, which is to be accounted for by the healthfulness of the climate and by its being a rich and prosperous farming section, where negroes were well fed and probably free from the malarial ailments of some other sections. The conditions, therefore, were very favorable to the prolific negro race.

We think it would be only natural that one should expect to have found in Virginia and

[16]For data upon which these arguments are based see Census Reports of 1830, 1840, and 1860.

Maryland, which have had to bear the brunt of the accusation of breeding slaves, the greatest proportion of children; not only because of the reiterated accusations, but also on account of the exportation of adult slaves from these States, which had the tendency to heighten the proportion of children in these States and lessen it in the States to which slaves were carried.

With regard to slave breeding, Shaffner, a native of Virginia, says: "From our own personal observation, since we were capable of studying the progress of human affairs, we are of opinion that there is less increase of the slaves of the so-called 'breeding States,' than of the more Southern of Gulf States."[17]   "We doubt if there exists in America a slave owner that encourages the breeding of slaves for the purpose of selling them.   Nor do we believe that any man would be permitted to live in any of the Southern States that did intentionally breed slaves with the object of selling them.[18]

Southerners generally have denied the accusa-

[17]Shaffner: The War in America, p. 256.
[18]Ibid., p. 296.

tion. When Andrew Stevenson, of Virginia, was minister to England, he was, upon one occasion, taunted by Daniel O'Connell with belonging to a State that was noted for breeding slaves for the South. He indignantly denied the charge.[19] And in 1839 the editor of the "Cincinnati Gazette" was much abused for asserting that Virginia bred slaves as a matter of pecuniary gain.[20]

Nehemiah Adams, a clergyman, went South in the early fifties biased against slavery, but says, "the charge of vilely multiplying negroes in Virginia is one of those exaggerations of which the subject is full, and is reduced to this: that Virginia being an old State fully stocked, the surplus black population naturally flows off where their numbers are less.[21]

It would seem that these States are not only practically freed from the charge of multiplying slaves and raising them for market as a business, but that, as a rule, they did not sell their slaves

---

[19] Annual Report of Am. and Foreign Anti-Slavery Society, 1850, p. 108.

[20] Ibid.

[21] Nehemiah Adams: Southern View of Slavery, p. 78.

unless compelled to do so by pecuniary or other embarrassments.

Probably many planters were as conscientious about their slaves as Jefferson appears to have been. In a letter he says:

"I cannot decide to sell my lands. I have sold too much of them already, and they are the only sure provision for my children, nor would I willingly sell the slaves as long as their remains any prospect of paying my debts with their labor."[22]

It seems that he was finally compelled to sell some of them.[23] Madison parted with some of his best land to feed the increasing numbers of negroes, but admitted to Harriet Martineau that the week before she visited him he had been obliged to sell a dozen of them.[24] And Estwick Evans, who made a long tour of the country in 1818, says, "I know it to be a case, that slave holders, generally, deprecate the practice of buy-

[22]Ford: Jefferson's Works.   Vol. VI., pp. 416-417.
[23]Ford: Jeff. Works. Vol. VI., p. 214.
[24]Martineau: Retrospect of Western Travel, Vol. II., p. 5.

ing and selling slaves."[25]   No doubt, the planters were always glad to get rid of unruly and good-for-nothing negroes, and these were pretty sure to fall into the hands of traders.[26]   The slave traders had agents spread over the States, where slaves were less profitable to their owners, in readiness to take advantage of every opportunity to secure the slaves that might in any way be for sale.   They would, even when an opportunity occurred, kidnap the free negroes.   They also sought to buy up slaves as if for local and domestic use and then would disappear with them.[27] And it was a common occurrence for plantations and negroes to be advertised for sale.   In one issue of the "Charleston Courier" in the winter of 1835 were advertised several plantations and about 1,200 negroes for sale.[28]   At such sales negro traders and speculators from far and near were sure to be on hand attracted by the prospect of making good bargains.[29]

[25]Evans: A Pedestrious Tour, p. 216.
[26]Olmsted: Seaboard Slave States, p. 392.
[27]Reed and Matheson: Narrative of a Visit to the American Churches, Vol. II., p. 173.
[28]Charleston Courier (S. C.), Feb. 12, 1835.
[29]Sequel to Mrs. Kemble's Journal, p. 1 (Yale)

Probably we could not better close this chapter than with a quotation from Dr. Baily, who was editor of the "National Era," a moderate anti-slavery paper. It appears to us that he correctly and concisely sums up the whole matter:

"The sale of slaves to the South," he says, "is carried on to a great extent. The slave holders do not, so far as I can learn, raise them for that special purpose. But here is a man with a score of slaves, located on an exhausted plantation. It must furnish support for all; but while they increase, its capacity of supply decreases. The result is he must emancipate or sell. But he has fallen into debt, and he sells to relieve himself of debt and also from the excess of mouths. Or he requires money to educate his children; or his negroes are sold under execution. From these and other causes, large numbers of slaves are continually disappearing from the State. . . .

"The Davises in Petersburg are the great slave dealers. They are Jews, who came to that place many years ago as poor peddlers. . . . These

Slavery Pamphlet, Vol. XVII. De Bow's Review, Vol. XXIV., p. 595. Liberator, Sept. 7, 1860; also May 6, 1853.

men are always in the market, giving the highest price for slaves. During the summer and fall they buy them up at low prices, trim, shave, wash them, fatten them so that they may look sleek and sell them to great profit. . . .

"There are many planters who cannot be persuaded to sell their slaves. They have far more than they can find work for, and could at any time obtain a high price for them. The temptation is strong for they want more money and fewer dependents. But they resist it, and nothing can induce them to part with a single slave, though they know that they would be greatly the gainers in a pecuniary sense, were they to sell one-half of them."[30]

---

[30]National Era, June 10, 1847.

CHAPTER V.

THE KIDNAPPING AND SELLING OF FREE NEGROES INTO SLAVERY.

VIRGINIA, as early as 1753, enacted a law against importation of free negroes for sale and stealing of slaves.[1] In 1788 another law was passed against kidnapping. It recited that several evil-disposed persons had seduced or stolen children or mulatto and black free persons ; and that there was no law adequate for such offenses. This law made the penalty for such a crime very severe. Upon conviction the offender was to suffer death without benefit of clergy.[2] North Carolina had already (1779) enacted a law, with the same penalty, against stealing slaves and kidnapping free negroes.[3]

The other Southern States which had laws

---

[1] Hening : Statutes at Large, Vol. VI., p. 357.

[2] Ibid., Vol. XII., p. 531.

[3] Laws of State of North Carolina. Revised Under Authority of the General Assembly, Vol. I., p. 375.

against kidnapping are: Alabama,[4] Maryland,[5] Mississippi,[6] Missouri,[7] Florida,[8] South Carolina,[9] Arkansas,[10] Tennessee,[11] Louisiana,[12] Georgia.[13] Delaware, however, had the most interesting as well as very severe laws against kidnapping. That of 1793 required that any one guilty of kidnapping or of assisting to kidnap free negroes or mulattoes should be whipped with thirty-nine lashes on the bare back, and stand in the pillory with both of his ears nailed to it,

[4]Acts of General Assembly of Alabama, 1840-41, p. 125.

[5]Maxcy: Revised Laws of Maryland, Vol. II., p. 356 (1811). Dorsey: General Public Statuary Law, Vol. I., p. 112.

[6]Hutchinson: Code of Mississippi (1798 to 1848), p. 960. Revised Code of Mississippi, Authority of Legislature (1857), p. 603.

[7]Laws of State of Missouri Revised by Legislature (1825), Vol. I., p. 289.

[8]Laws of Florida, 1850-51, p. 132-3.

[9]Laws of South Carolina, 1837. p. 58.

[10]English: Digest of Statutes of Arkansas (1848) Authority of Leg. Chap. LI., p. 333.

[11]Hurd: Law of Freedom and Bondage, Vol. II., p. 92.

[12]Laws of a Public and General Nature of the District of Louisiana, of Territory of Louisiana and Territory of Missouri and State of Missouri to 1824 (passed Oct. 1, 1804).

[13]Hurd: Vol. II., p. 106.

and when he came out to have their soft parts
cut off.[14] In 1826 the penalties were made even
more severe: $1,000 fine, pillory one hour, to be
whipped with sixty lashes upon the bare back,
to be imprisoned from three to seven years, at
the expiration of which he was to be disposed of
as a servant for seven years, and upon second
conviction to suffer death.[15] In 1831 Congress
passed a law to prevent the abduction and sale
of free negroes from the District of Columbia.[16]

It is quite evident from these laws that kidnapping was a very common crime. It does not
appear, however, that they prevented it.

Even as early as 1817 it was estimated by Torrey, who seems to have made a study of the subject, that several thousand legally free persons
were toiling in servitude, having been kidnapped.[17]

Free negro children were the ones who were

---

[14]Laws of State of Delaware, Oct. 14, 1793. Hurd,
Vol. IV. p. 76.

[15]Passed Feb. 8, 1826. Laws of Delaware, Vol. VI.,
p. 715.

[16]Statutes at Large, Vol. V., p. 450.

[17]Jessie Torrey: A Portraiture of Domestic Slavery,
p. 57.

most liable to be kidnapped,[18] for the reason
probably that they were easier managed and less
likely to have about them proofs of their freedom, though sometimes, indeed, even white children, whether being mistaken for negroes or not,
were stolen and sold into slavery.[19]

More than twenty free colored children were
kidnapped in Philadelphia in 1825.[20] It is stated
that some persons gained a livelihood by stealing negroes from the towns of the North and
carrying them to the South for sale.[21] Statements similar to the following are often to be
met with in the papers published in slavery
times:

"Four negro children, 18, 17, 9 and 5 years
respectively—first two girls; last two boys—
were kidnapped and carried off from Gallatin

---

[18]An address to the People of North Carolina, p. 38.
(Y.) Sl. Pamp., Vol. LXI.
    Liberator: May 18, 1849. Niles' Reg., Feb. 25, 1826.
[19]Emancipator, March 8, 1848.

[20]Mrs. Childs: Anti-Slavery Catechism, p. 14. (Yale)
Slavery Pamp., Vol. LXII.

[21]Buckingham: The Eastern and Western States of
America, Vol. I., p. 11. Niles' Reg., Oct. 18, 1828.
Liberator, Oct. 1, 1852, Aug. 14, 1857. Alexander,
Transatlantic Sketches, p. 230.

88   The Domestic Slave Trade

County, Illinois, on the evening of 5 ult. The
father . . . was tied while the children
were taken away. The kidnapping gang is regularly organized and is increasing. The mem-
bers are well known but cannot be punished on
account of the disqualification of negroes as witnesses."[22]

"About midnight on the 27th of September
a party of 8 or 10 Kentuckians broke into the
house of a Mr. Powell, in Cass County, Michi-
gan, while he was absent. They drew their pistols and bowie knives and dragged his wife and
three children from their beds, and bound them
with cords and hurried them off to their covered
wagons and started post haste for Kentucky."[23]

Probably kidnapping was carried on even more
extensively in the slave States themselves. "The

---

[22]Liberator, May 18, 1849.

[23]Ibid., Nov. 23, 1849. *Other cases*: Liberator, July
31, 1846; Sept. 5, 1845; Oct. 1, 1852; Dec. 3, 1841; Aug.
11, 1857; Aug. 15, 1856; April 25, 1835; Jan. 10, 1835;
May 7, 1835; Nov. 6, 1846; Niles' Reg., Sept. 27, 1817;
Jan. 31, 1818; May 23, 1818; July 4, 1818; Dec. 12,
1818; Feb. 25, 1826; June 28, 1828. W. Faux, Memorable Days in America, p. 277. Several of these as given
took place in slave States.

Liberator," quoting from the "Denton (Md.) Journal" in 1849 says:

"Three free negro youths, a girl and two boys, were kidnapped and taken from the County with intent to sell them to the South. . . . They had been hired for a few days by Mr. James T. Wooters, near Denton, for the ostensible purpose of cutting cornstalks. After being a day or two in Mr. Wooters' employ they suddenly disappeared. . . . Enquiry being set on foot, it was, after some days discovered that they had been secretly carried through Hunting Creek towards Worcester County, thence to Virginia. We learn that the Negroes are now in Norfolk."[24]

They were carried to Richmond where they were sold as slaves, but were finally recovered.[25]

Notwithstanding the harshness of the Delaware laws against kidnapping and the convictions[26] under them, the business of kidnapping seems to have flourished there. A quotation or two will illustrate:

"Two young colored men, free born, were

[24]Liberator, April 27, 1849.
[25]Ibid, June 8, 1849.
[26]North Carolina Standard, June 21, 1837.
    Niles' Register, April 25, 1829.

stolen from Wilmington a few nights ago and taken, it is supposed, to some of the Southern slave markets. . . . Fifty or sixty persons it is said, have been stolen from the lower part of the State in the last six months."[27]

In 1840 the "Baltimore Sun" said: "A most villainous system of kidnapping has been extensively carried on in the State of Delaware by a gang of scoundrels residing there, aided and abetted by a number of confederates living on the Eastern Shore of this State."[28]

While discussing kidnapping in Delaware, it is very unlikely we should forget to mention probably the most notorious kidnapping gang which the domestic slave trade produced. The principal character of the gang, and the one from which it seems to have drawn its inspiration, and the one from which it took its name—was a woman—in looks more like a man than a woman— Patty Cannon by name—well known by tradition

---

[27]The Christian Citizen, Dec. 21, 1844. Quoting from Penn. Freeman.

[28]Liberator, Feb. 21, 1840.

to every Delawarian and Eastern Shore of Mary-
lander. A son-in-law of hers was hanged for the
murder of a negro trader. His widow then married one Joe Johnson who became a noted character in the business of kidnapping through the
aid and instruction of his mother-in-law, Patty
Cannon. Johnson was convicted once and suf-
fered the punishment of the lash and pillory.
The grand jury in May, 1829, found three indict-
ments for murder against Patty Cannon,[29] but
she died in jail May 11, of the same year.[30]

White kidnappers sometimes used free colored
men as tools by means of which to ensnare other
free colored men, and shared with them the

---

[29]Niles' Weekly Reg., April 25, 1829. Quoting from
Del. Gazette of April 17. American Annual Register,
1827-8-9, Vol. III., p. 123.

[30]Niles' Register, May 23, 1829.
  Note on P. Cannon. George Alfred Townsend
wrote a romance of about 700 pages, entitled "The En-
tailed Hat, or Patty Cannon's Times," in which Patty
Cannon is one of the principal characters. It is a very
interesting and instructive story. Townsend was a
native of Delaware and well qualified to write such a
story. He says in the introduction: "Often had she
told him of old Patty Cannon and her kidnapping den
and her death in the jail of his native town. He found
the legend of that dreaded woman had strengthened
instead of having faded with time, and her haunts pre-
served, and eye witnesses of her deeds to be still living.

profits of the trade.[31]   Indeed, the free colored
men seem not to have been much averse in aiding
in the enslavement of their "brethren."   They
sometimes even formed kidnapping bands of their
own and pursued the business without the aid
of white men.   Such a gang as this once operated
near Snow Hill, Maryland.   It is said to have
kidnapped and sent off several hundred free
negroes.[32]

Kidnappers devised various schemes for the
accomplishment of their purposes, some of them
no less humorous than infamous.   A man in
Philadelphia was found to be engaged in the occupation of courting and marrying mulatto wo-

----

"Hence, this romance has much local truth in it
and is not only the narrative of an episode, but the
story of a large region, comprehending three State
jurisdictions."
    " 'Patty Cannon's dead; they say she's took poison.'
    "A mighty pain seized the Chancellor's heart, and
the loud groans he made called a stranger into the
room.
    " 'Is that dreadful woman dead?' sighed the Chan-
cellor.
    " 'Yes; she will never plague Delaware again, Mar-
ster.'
    " 'God be thanked!' the old man groaned."
    "Entailed Hat," p. 541.
    [31]Liberator: Sept. 14, 1849; Jan. 10, 1835.
    [32]Niles' Register, April 10, 1824; Oct. 10, 1818.

men and then selling them as slaves.[33]   Another
plan was for one or two confederates to find out
the bodily marks of a suitable free colored person after which the other confederate would go
before a magistrate and lay claim to the ill-fated
negro, describing his marks, call in his accomplice
as witness and so get possession of the negroes.[34]

Probably the most ingenious of all methods
of kidnapping was that brought to light in
Charleston, South Carolina, as related by Francis
Hall :

"The agents were a justice of the peace, a constable and a slave dealar. . . . A victim
having been selected, one of the firm applied to
the justice upon a shown charge of assault, or
similar offense, for a writ, which was immediately
issued and served by the constable, and the negro
conveyed to prison. . . . The constable
now appears, exaggerates the dangers of his situ-
ation, explains how small is his chance of being
liberated even if innocent, by reason of the

---

[33]Jessie Torrey: A Portraiture of Domestic Slavery, p. 57.

[34]Ibid.

amount of jail fees and other legal expenses; but
he knows a worthy man who is interested in his
behalf, and will do what is necessary to procure
his freedom upon no harder condition than an
agreement to serve him for a certain number of
years. It may be supposed the negro is persuaded.   .   .   .   The worthy slave dealer now appears on the stage, the indenture of bondage is
ratified in the presence of the worthy magistrate
and the constable, who shares the price of blood,
and the victim is hurried on shipboard to be seen
no more."[35]

From the nature of our information concerning
kidnapping it is readily seen that we have but
little basis for a statistical estimate of the number kidnapped. It must have ranged, however,
from a few hundred to two or three thousand
annually. It appears quite certain that as many
were kidnapped as escaped from bondage, if not
more.

The "Liberator" alone records nearly a hundred cases of detected kidnapping between 1831

---

[35]Francis Hall: Travels in Canada and the United
States, p. 425.

and 1860.   But the number detected probably
bears but little relation to the number actually
kidnapped.   As was before shown in the cases
mentioned almost whole families were carried
off, and that in most cases, when a discovery was
made, it was found that the kidnapping gang
had been in the business for years.

CHAPTER VI.

SLAVE "PRISONS," MARKETS, CHARACTER OF TRAD-
DERS, ETC.

In all the large towns and cities were slave "prisons" or "pens"[1] in which slaves were kept until enough for a drove or shipment could be collected.[2] The slave prisons ranged all the way from a rude whitewashed shed[3] to large and commodious establishments accommodating hundreds of slaves. A description of one of these—The Franklin and Armfield prison which was in Alexandria—by Andrews is rather interesting:

"The establishment," he says, . . . "is situated in a retired quarter in the southern part of the city. It is easily distinguished as you approach it, by the high, whitewashed wall sur-

---

[1]Featherstonhaugh: Excursion Through the Slave States, Vol. I., p. 128.

[2]Liberator: Feb. 16, 1833. Buckingham: Slave States, Vol. II., p. 485.

[3]Reed and Matheson: Visit to Am. Churches, Vol. I., p. 32.

rounding the yards and giving to it the appearance of a penitentiary. The dwelling house is of brick, three stories high, and opening directly upon the street; over the front door is the name of the firm. . . .

"We passed out of the back door of the dwelling house and entered a spacious yard nearly surrounded with neatly whitewashed two story buildings, devoted to the use of the slaves. Turning to the left we came to a strong grated door of iron opening into a spacious yard surrounded by a high whitewashed wall, one side of this yard was roofed, but the principal part was open to the air. Along the covered side extended a table, at which the slaves had recently taken their dinner, which, judging from what remained, had been wholesome and abundant. . . . The gate was secured by strong padlocks and bolts."[4]

Such was the slave prison of one of the largest and most prosperous slave-dealing firms.

There were many dealers who had no place of their own in which to keep slaves, but were de-

---

[4]Andrews: Slavery and the Domestic Slave Trade, pp. 135-7.

pendent upon the "prisons" of others.[5]   Indeed, at Washington, the city public prison was often used by negro traders as a place of safety for their slaves. The keeper was paid by the traders for the privilege.[6] This practice continued a great number of years. In 1843 the poet Whittier thus describes the prison:

"It is a damp, dark and loathsome building. We passed between two ranges of small stone cells filled with blacks. We noticed five or six in a single cell which seemed scarcely large enough for a solitary tenant. The heat was suffocating. In rainy weather the keeper told us that the prison was uncomfortably wet. In winter there could be no fire in these cells. The keeper with some reluctance admitted that he received negroes from the traders and kept them until they were sold, at thirty-four cents per day."[7]

While, no doubt, some traders kept their "prisons" in as good condition[8] as circumstances

[5]Sturge: A Visit to the United States, p. 107.
[6]Miner: Speech in Congress, Jan. 6, 1829.
   Gales and Seaton's Register of Debates in Congress, Vol. V., p. 167.
[7]Whittier: A Letter in Emancipator, Nov. 23, 1843.
[8]Andrews: Slavery and the Domestic Trade, p. 164.

would allow, there were others, and probably the majority, who did not. A Northern minister describes those at Richmond in 1845, as "mostly filthy and loathsome places."[9]

In the buying States two of the principal slave markets were Natchez and New Orleans.[10] That of Natchez is thus described about 1835 by Ingraham:

"A mile from Natchez we come to a cluster of rough wooden buildings, in the angle of two roads in front of which several saddle horses, either tied or held by servants, indicated a place of popular resort. . . . We entered through a wide gate into a narrow court yard. A line of negroes extended in a semicircle around the right side of the yard. There were in all about forty. Each was dressed in the usual uniform when in market consisting of a fashionably shaped black fur hat, . . . trousers of coarse corduroy velvet, good vests, strong shoes, and white cotton shirts."[11] . . .

---

[9]Christian Freeman, Sept. 10, 1845.
[10]African Repository, Vol. V., p. 381, cited from Mercantile Advertiser of New Orleans, Jan. 21, 1830.
Tower: Slavery Unmasked, p. 304.
[11](Ingraham): The Southwest, Vol. II., p. 192.

"There are four or five markets in the vicinity of Natchez. Several hundred slaves of all ages are exposed to sale. . . . Two extensive markets for slaves opposite each other, on the road to Washington three miles from Natchez."[12]

A slave market in New Orleans was described in 1844 as a large and splendidly decorated edifice, which had the appearance of having been fitted up as a place of recreation. It had a number of apartments, a handsome archway, and a large green lawn or outer court "beautifully decorated with trees." In this lawn the sale of slaves was held.[13]

When a trader in the selling States had collected enough for a shipment or "coffle" they were sent to the markets in the buying States.[14] Slaves were sent South both by land and water.[15] In the

---

[12]Ibid., p. 201.

[13]Christian Freeman, Jan. 2, 1845; quoted from Western Citizen by C. F.

[14]Buckingham: Slave States of Am. II., p. 485.
Liberator, Feb. 16, 1833. Abdy: Journal of a Residence in the United States, Vol. II., p. 100.

[15]Andrews: Sl. and the Domestic Sl. Trade, p. 142.

winter they were usually sent by water, but in summer they were often sent by land.[16]

In the transportation of slaves the utmost precautions were necessary to prevent revolt or escape.[17] When a "coffle" or "drove" was formed to undertake its march of seven or eight weeks to the South[18] the men would be chained,—"two by two, and a chain passing through the double file and fastening from the right and left hands of those on either side of the chain."[19]

This seems to have been the usual method of securing them. The purpose was to have the men so completely bound as to render escape or resistance impossible. The girls, children and women usually were not chained and even sometimes rode in the wagons which accompanied the

---

[16]Ibid.: p. 78.
   Buckingham: Slave States, Vol. II., p. 485.
   Liberator, Feb. 16, 1833.
   Featherstonhaugh: Excursion Through the Slave States, Vol. I., p. 120.
[17]Niles' Reg., Sept. 5. 1829.
   Featherstonhaugh: Excursion Through the Slave States, Vol. I., p. 122.
   Niles' Reg., Oct. 14, 1826; Nov. 18, 1826; May 20, 1826.
[18](Ingraham): The Southwest, Vol. II., p. 238.
[19]Adams: Southern View of Slavery, p. 77.

train.[20] The "droves" were conducted by white
men, usually, on horseback and well armed with
pistols[21] and whips.[22]

The negroes were usually well fed on their
way South and when they arrived at their desti-
nation, though their personal appearance was not
improved, they were generally stouter and in better condition than when they began their march.
Pains was now taken to have them polish their
skins and dress themselves in the uniform suits
provided for the purpose.[23] Then they were ready
for market. At the sale the auctioneer would de-
scant at large upon the merits and capabilities of
the subject.[24] The slave, too, often would enter
into a display of his physical appearance with as

[20]The Christian Citizen, Oct. 26, 1844.
  Featherstonhaugh: Excursion Through the Slave
States, Vol. I., pp. 120-122.
  Palmer: Journal of Travels in the U. S., p. 142.
  Birkbeck: Notes on a Journey from the Coast of
Va., p. 25.
[21](Paulding): Letters From the South, Vol. I., p.
128. (Ed. 1817.)
[22]Buckingham: Slave States of America, Vol. II., p.
533.
  (Blane): An Excursion Through the U. S. and
Canada, p. 226.
[23](Ingraham): The Southwest, Vol. II., p. 238.
[24]Ibid.: Vol. II., p. 30.

much apparent earnestness to command a high price as though he were to share the profits. He would seem to enjoy a spirited bidding.[25] Each negro wished to be sold first as it was thought by them to be an evidence of superiority.[26]

At the sales and auctions the purchaser was allowed the greatest freedom in the examination of the slaves for sale. And he would scrutinize them as carefully as though they were horses or cattle. The teeth, eyes, feet and shoulders of both men and women were inspected, sometimes without any show of decency.[27] Scars or marks of the lash decreased their value in market, sometimes the sale would be lost for that reason.[28]

In the slave trade there is no doubt that families were often separated.[29] Though Andrews tells of a trader sending a lot of mothers without their

[25] Ashworth: A Tour in the U. S., Cuba and Canada, p. 81; also Sequel to Mrs. Kemble's Journal, p. 8 in (Y.) Sl. Pamp., Vol. XVII.
  (Ingraham): The Southwest, Vol. II., p. 201.
[26] (Ingraham): The Southwest, Vol. II., p. 201.
[27] Christian Freeman: April 10, 1845.
  Christian Citizen, Nov. 23, 1844.
[28] Shaffner: The War in America, p. 293.
[29] Tower: Slavery Unmasked, p. 127-8.
  Andrews: Sl. and Domestic Slave Trade, p. 105.

children in such a way as to lead one to believe such a case was exceptional.[30] Negroes on large plantations were sometimes advertised to be sold in families.[31]

Nehemiah Adams says that in settling estates in the South "good men exercise as much care with regard to the disposition of slaves as though they were providing for white orphan children. . . . Slaves are allowed to find masters and mistresses who will buy them."[32]

Another traveller in speaking of the slave auction at Natchez, says:

"It is a rule seldom deviated from, to sell families and relations together, if practicable. A negro trader in my presence refused to sell a negro girl for whom a planter offered a high price because he would not also purchase her sister."[33]

As a rule negroes had a great dislike to be sold South; in the early history of the trade this

---

[30]Andrews: Slavery and Domestic Sl. Trade, p. 164.

[31]Liberator, May 6. 1853.
Sequel to Mrs. Kemble's Journal, p. 11. in (Yale) Sl. Pamp., Vol. XVII.

[32]Adams: Southern View of Slavery, p. 72.

[33](Ingraham) : The Southwest, Vol. II., p. 201.

amounted to horror for them.[34] Whether this dislike arose from the impression that they might not
be treated so well or simply from the natural
dislike of removing to a strange land is a question,
though the latter seems much more probable.[35]
In 1835, however, it appears that the Virginia
slaves were not so averse to going South for the
reason that many who had gone there sent back
such favorable accounts of their circumstances.[36]

Another phase of the domestic slave trade,
which it may not be out of way to mention, was
the traffic in beautiful mulatto or quadroon girls.
It was a part of the slave trader's business to
search out and obtain them. At New Orleans,
or elsewhere, they were sold at very high prices
for the purpose of prostitution or as mistresses.[37]

From a letter written in 1850 by a slave dealer

---

[34] (Paulding) : Letters from the South, Vol. I., p.
126: (Ed. 1817).
Torrey: A Portraiture of Domestic Slavery in
U. S., p. 145.
[35] Olmsted: Cotton Kingdom, Vol. I., p. 336.
[36] Andrews: Slavery and Domestic Sl. Trade, p. 118.
[37] Candler: A Summary View of Am., p. 276.
Liberator, June 18, 1847.
(Blane) : Excursion Through the U. S., p. 209.
Tower: Slavery Unmasked, p. 304-7.

of Alexandria, Virginia, we quote the following:

"We . . . cannot afford to sell the girl Emily for less than $1,800. . . . We have two or three offers for Emily from gentlemen from the South. She is said to be the finest looking woman in this country.[38]

In New Orleans they often brought very high prices. The "Liberator" quoting from the New York "Sun" in 1837 concerning the sale of a girl at New Orleans, says: "The beautiful Martha was struck off at $4,500."[39] And in the New Orleans "Picayune," of the same year, was an account of a girl—"remarkable for her beauty and intelligence"—who sold at $7,000 in New Orleans.[40] Many other instances might be given but we think these sufficient.

A word now with reference to slave traders and the general estimation in which they were held in the South.

Ingraham says: "Their admission into society . . . is not recognized. Planters associate

---

[38]Stowe: Key to Uncle Tom's Cabin, p. 169.
[39]Liberator, July 7, 1837.
[40]Quarterly Anti-Slavery Magazine, Vol. II., p. 409, July, 1837.

with them freely enough, in the way of business, but notice them no further. A slave trader is much like other men. He is to-day a plain farmer with twenty or thirty slaves endeavoring to earn a few dollars from the worn out land, in some old homestead. He is in debt and hears he can sell his slaves in Mississippi for twice their value in his own State. He takes his slaves and goes to Mississippi. He finds it profitable and his inclinations prompt him to buy of his neighbors when he returns home and makes another trip to Mississippi, thus he gets started."[41]

Some traders were no doubt honorable men. Indeed, Andrews gives us a very pleasing picture of Armfield, the noted Alexandria, Virginia, slave dealer. He describes him as "a man of fine personal appearance, and of engaging and graceful manners."[42] . . . "Nothing, however, can reconcile the moral sense of the Southern public to

---

[41](Ingraham) : The Southwest, Vol. II., p. 245.

[42]Andrews: Slavery and the Domestic Slave Trade, pp. 136, 150.

Note:—It is interesting to compare Featherstonhaugh's characterization of Armfield, which is: "I looked steadily at the fellow, and recollecting him, found no longer any difficulty in accounting for such a

the character of a trader in slaves. However
honorable may be his dealings his employment
is accounted infamous."[43]

Upon the whole, no doubt the characterization
of the slave traders by Featherstonhaugh was a
true one:

"Sordid, illiterate and vulgar . . . men who
have nothing whatever in common with the gen-
tlemen of the Southern States."[44]

Finch says: "A slave dealer is considered the
lowest and most degraded occupation, and none
will engage in it unless they have no other means
of support."[45]

Indeed it seems they were accounted the abhor-
rence of every one. Their descendants, when
known, had a blot upon them and the property
acquired in the traffic as well.[46]

---

compound of everything vulgar and revolting and totally without education. I had now a key to his manner and the expression of his countenance."—Featherstonhaugh: Excursion Through the Slave States, Vol.
I., p. 167.

[43]Andrews: Sl. and Domestic Sl. Trade, p. 150.

[44]Featherstonhaugh: Excursion Through the Slave
States, Vol. I., p. 128.

[45]Finch: Travels in the U. S. and Canada, p. 241.

[46]Adams: Southern View of Slavery, p. 77.

CHAPTER VII.

LAWS OF THE SOUTHERN STATES WITH REFERENCE
TO IMPORTATION AND EXPORTATION OF SLAVES.

VIRGINIA.

THE General Assembly of Virginia, 1778, enacted that "no slaves shall hereafter be imported
into this commonwealth, by sea or land, nor shall
any slave or slaves so imported be sold or bought
by any person whatever," under penalty of one
thousand pounds for every slave imported and five
hundred pounds for every one either sold or
bought, and the slave himself to be free. It was
provided, however, that persons removing to the
State from other States with the intention of becoming citizens of Virginia might bring their
slaves with them, upon taking the following oath
within ten days after their removal:

"I. A. B. do swear that my removal to the State
of Virginia was with no intention to evade the
act for preventing the further importation of

slaves within this commonwealth, nor have I brought with me. nor have any of the slaves now in my possession been imported from Africa, or any of the West India Islands since the first day of November 1778, so help me God."[1]

This act did not apply to persons claiming slaves by descent, marriage or divorce, or to any citizen of Virginia who was then the actual owner of slaves within any of the United States, nor to transient travellers having slaves as necessary attendants.[2]

In 1785 a law was passed declaring free the slaves who should afterward be imported and kept in the State a year, whether at one time or at several times. (a) The same exceptions were made as in the law of 1778.

In 1796 these acts were amended making it lawful for any citizen of the United States residing in Virginia or owning lands there to carry out any slaves born in the State and bring them back, provided they had neither been hired nor

---

[1] Hening: Statutes at Large, Vol. IX., p. 471.
[2] Hening: Vol. IX., p. 471. (a) Ibid., Vol. XII., p. 182.

sold. If, however, they were entitled to freedom
in the State to which they were removed, they
could not again be held as slaves in Virginia.[3]

In 1806 a law was passed totally prohibiting
the introduction of slaves into Virginia.[4] It was
amended, however, in 1811, in favor of residents
of the State, as it restored to them the same privi-
leges concerning the importation of slaves which
they had under the law of 1778.[5] An act of
January 9, 1813, further amended and extended to
immigrants the right of bringing in slaves. They
were allowed to introduce only such slaves as they
had owned for two years or acquired by marriage
or inheritance. Any one introducing slaves was
put under obligation not to sell them within two
years. Those thus importing slaves were required
also to exhibit before a justice of the peace a
written statement with the name, age, sex and description of each slave, and to take oath that the
account was true and that they were not introduced for the purpose of sale or with the inten-

---

[3]Shepherd: Statutes at Large, of Va., Vol. II., p. 19.
[4]Shepherd: Statutes at Large, Vol. III., p. 251.
[5]Acts of 1810-1811, p. 15, C. 14.

tion for evading the laws.[6] The last act of Virginia regarding the importation of slaves was that of 1819. This law permitted the importation of slaves not convicted of crime, from any of the United States.[7]

SOUTH CAROLINA.

In 1792 South Carolina passed a law to prohibit for two years the importation of slaves from Africa, or from "other places beyond the seas;" it also prohibited the introduction of slaves who were bound for a term of years in any of the United States. An exception, however, was made of citizens who might acquire slaves by marriage, or actual settlers in the State and of travellers.[8] This act was revised in 1794 and extended to 1797. As revised it totally prohibited the introduction of slaves into South Carolina from all places from without the United States.[9] In 1796

[6]Acts of the General Assembly of Va., 1812-13, p. 26, C. 28.
[7]Ibid., 1818-19, p. 37, C. 26.
[8]Faust: Acts of General Assembly of S. C. From 1791 to 1794, Vol. I., p. 215. McCord, Statutes at Large of S. C., Vol. VII., p. 431.
[9]Ibid., p. 444.

it was extended to 1799;[10] again extended in 1798
to 1801 (a) ; and in 1800 it was again extended
to 1803. In 1800, also, an act was passed totally
prohibiting the introduction of slaves into the
State except by immigrants,[11] and in 1801 it was
made even more stringent: Any slaves brought in
were to be sold by the sheriff of the district in
which they were found upon the order of the
court.[12] It was found that the acts of 1800 and
1801 were too rigorous and inconvenient. In
1802 that part of the laws which prevented citizens of other States from carrying their own
slaves through South Carolina was repealed. It
was provided that any one who wished to pass
through the State with slaves might do so; but
near the place where he was to enter the State
he should take the following oath before a magistrate or quorum :

"I, A. B., do swear that the slaves which I am
carrying through this State are bona fide my property, and that I will not sell, hire or dispose of

[9]McCord: Vol. VII., p. 433.
[10]Ibid.: p. 434   (a) p. 435.
[11]Ibid.: pp. 436-439.

said slaves, or either of them, to any resident or citizen, or body corporate or public, or any other person or persons whomsoever, within the State of South Carolina, but will travel directly to the place where I intend to move.[13]

In 1803 an act repealing and amending former acts on the importation of slaves was enacted. The introduction of negroes from the West Indies or South America was prohibited; and from any of the other States unless with a certificate of good character. There was no restriction with respect to Africa.[14]

No more laws regarding importation were passed until 1816. Then it was enacted that no slave should be brought into the State "from any of the United States or territories or countries bordering thereon." The only exception was in favor of travellers with not more than two slaves, or settlers on their way to other States, who, before entering South Carolina, were required to take an oath with regard to their slaves similar

---

[13]McCord: Stat. at Large of S. C., Vol. VII., p. 447.
[14]Ibid., p. 449.

to that required by the law of 1802.[15]   This law
was amended in 1817 in part as follows:

"That every inhabitant of this State who was
bona fide entitled in his or her own right or in the
right of his wife, to any slave or slaves on the
19th day of December, 1816, or hereafter shall
become entitled to any such slave, by inheritance
or marriage, shall be permitted to bring them in"
on certain conditions.[16] Both the law of 1816 and
that of 1817 were repealed in 1818.[17]

In 1823 South Carolina made it lawful to
bring into the State any slave from the "West
Indies, South America, or from Europe, or from
any sister State which may be situated to the
North of the Potomac River or the City of Washington."   No slave was allowed to return to
South Carolina who had been carried out of the
State and had visited any of these places.   The
penalty was severe, it being $1,000 and forfeiture
of the slave.[18]   This law was re-enacted in 1835,[19]

---

[15]Acts and Resolutions of the General Assembly of
S. C., 1816, p. 22.
[16]Acts of S. C., 1817, p. 17.
[17]Laws of South Carolina, 1818, p. 57.
[18]Ibid., 1823, p. 61.
[19]Ibid., 1835, p. 37.

and in 1847 it was amended to allow slaves to
return who should go to Cuba, on board of any
steamboat in the capacity of steward, cook, fire-
man, engineer, pilot, or mariner, provided he
had visited none of the other restricted places.[20]
It was amended again in 1848 and Baltimore
and all ports on the Chesapeake Bay in the State
of Maryland were placed on the same footing
with regard to the importation of slaves as the
States south of the Potomac.[21]

NORTH CAROLINA.

In 1786 North Carolina passed her first law
to restrict the importation of slaves from other
States. It was as follows:

"Every person who shall introduce into this
State any slave from any of the United States,
which have passed laws for the liberation of
slaves, shall, on complaint thereof before any
justice of the peace be compelled by such justice
to enter into bond with sufficient surety, in the sum
of $100 current money for each slave, for the re-
moving of such slave to the State from whence

[24]Ibid., 1848, Dec. 19, 1848.
[21]Laws of S. C., 1848, Dec. 19, 1848.

such slave was brought, within three months thereafter, the penalty to be recovered, one-half for the use of the State, the other half for the use of the prosecutor, or failure of a compliance therewith; and the person introducing such slave shall also, in case of such failure, forfeit and pay the sum of $200, to be recovered by any person suing for the same and applied to their use."[22]

A law of 1794 prohibited the introduction of slaves and indentured servants of color. Exceptions were made of slave owners coming to the States to reside and of citizens of North Carolina inheriting slaves in other States.[23] In 1795 emigrants from the West Indies, Bahama Islands, French, Dutch and Spanish settlements on the southern coast of America, were prevented from bringing in slaves who were more than fif-

---

[22]Revised Statutes, by Authority of the General Assembly, 1836-7, Vol. II., p. 575. Chap. III., Sec. 19. We could not find that it was ever repealed. It is to be found in the Revised Code of North Carolina, 1854. As this was taken from the Revised Statutes of 1836-7, it is natural to find the penalty expressed in dollars, rather than in pounds.

[23]Hayward: A Manual of the Laws of N. C., to 1817 inclusive, p. 533. Must have been repealed between 1817 and 1819, as it is not in the Revised Statutes of 1819.

teen years of age. An act of 1776, however, allowed slaves to be brought in who belonged
to residents near the Virginia and South Carolina
boundaries.[24] A law was passed in 1816 which
provided that slaves brought into North Carolina
from foreign countries contrary to the act of
Congress of 1807, to be sold. No more laws
concerning importation were passed after the re-
peal of the laws against importation about 1818.[23]

GEORGIA.

Georgia passed a law against the importation
of slaves in 1793.[25] This seemed to apply only
to slaves imported from without the United
States. In 1798 a new constitution was framed
which provided "that there shall be no importation of slaves into this State from Africa
or any foreign place after the first of October
next."[26]

In 1817 the following was enacted:

"It shall not be lawful, except in cases herein

---

[24]Hurd: Law of Freedom and Bondage, Vol. II., p. 84.
[25]Hurd: Freedom and Bondage, Vol. II., p. 101.
[26]Poore: Fed. and State Constitutions, Part I., p. 395.

authorized and allowed for any person or persons
whatever to bring, import or introduce into this
State, to aid, or assist, or knowingly to become
concerned or interested in bringing, importing
or introducing into this State, either by land or
by water, or in any manner whatsoever, any
slave or slaves." Citizens of Georgia and those
of other States coming to Georgia to live were
permitted to bring in slaves for their own use.
Before importing them they were required to
make oath before the proper authorities that they
were not imported for sale, or hire, lend, or mort-
gage. The act was not to extend to travellers.[27]
This act was repealed in 1824 and slaves then
were imported and disposed of without restriction.[28] The law of 1817 was revised in 1829;
modified in 1836; again repealed in 1841; revived again in 1842.[29]

In 1835 a law was enacted making any one
subject to fine and imprisonment who should
bring into Georgia any male slave who had been

---

[27]Acts of General Assembly of Ga., 1817, p. 139.
[28]Ibid., 1824, p. 124.
[29]Hurd: Law of Freedom and Bondage, Vol. II., p.
103.

to a non-slave-holding State or to any foreign
country.[30]

In 1849 "all laws and parts of laws, civil and
criminal, forbidding or in any manner restricting
the importation of slaves into this State from any
other slave-holding State" were repealed. Cities
and towns were given the right to regulate the
sale of slaves by traders, and to prescribe the
places in their jurisdiction where slaves might
be kept and sold.[31] In 1852 so much of this law
as had reference to importation of slaves was
repealed and the act of 1817 was revived.[32] But
the penitentiary imprisonment clause was elimi-
nated. The law of 1852 was repealed by the
Legislature of 1855-6 and the act of 1849 was
revived thus again opening the State to the unre-
stricted importation of slaves.[33]

MARYLAND.

In 1783 Maryland prohibited the importation
of slaves. It was amended in 1791 and also in

---

[30]Acts of the State of Ga., 1835, p. 267.
[31]Laws of Ga., 1849-50, p. 374.
[32]Acts of Ga., 1851-2, p. 263.
[33]Acts of Ga., 1855-6, p. 271.

1794.[34]   In 1796 the General Assembly of Maryland enacted: "That it shall not be lawful, from
and after the passing of this act to import or
bring into this State, by land or water, any negro,
mulatto, or other slave, for sale, or to reside
within this State; and any person brought into
this State as a slave contrary to this act, if a slave
before, shall thereupon immediately cease to be
the property of the person or persons so importing or bringing such slave within the State, and
shall be free."

Immigrants to the State were allowed to bring
in their own slaves, at the time of removal or
within one year afterward. It was required that
these slaves should have been within the United
States three years.[35]   In 1797 this law was modified in favor of those coming into Maryland to reside.   In 1810 a law was passed to prevent those
who were slaves for a limited time from being
sold out of the State.[36]

---

[34]Hurd: Law of Freedom and Bondage, Vol. II., p. 19.
[35]Maxcy: The Laws of Md., Vol. II., p. 351.   Co. 67.
Hurd: Vol. II., p. 21.
[36]Ibid.: 1897, Chap. 15.   Other exceptions by Public
and Private Acts, 1798, C. 76; 1812, C. 76; 1813, C.
55; 1818-19, C. 201; Hurd: Vol. II., p. 19.

In 1817 a law was passed regulating the ex-portation of slaves as follows:

"That whenever any person shall purchase any slave or slaves within this State, for the pur-pose of exporting or removing the same beyond the limits of this State, it shall be their duty to take from the seller a bill of sale for said slave or slaves, in which the age and distinguishing marks as nearly as may be, and the name of such slave or slaves shall be inserted and the same shall be acknowledged before some justice of the peace of the county where the sale shall be made and lodged to be recorded in the office of the clerk of the said county, within twenty days, and the clerk shall immediately on the receipt thereof, actually record the same and deliver a copy thereof on demand to the purchaser, with a cer-tificate endorsed thereupon under the seal of the county of the same being duly recorded."[37]

The following year (1818) a law was passed which provided that any slave convicted of a crime, which, in the judgment of the court should

---

[37]Dorsey: General Laws of Md., 1692 to 1839, Vol. I., p. 661.

not be punished by hanging, might be transported for sale.[38] In 1846 the legislature enacted that slaves, sentenced to the penitentiary should be publicly sold at the expiration of their service and transported.[39]

In 1831 a very restrictive law was enacted. It prohibited the introduction of slaves into the State either for sale or residence.[40] The restrictive policy did not continue long, for in 1833 the barrier to the introduction of slaves for residence was withdrawn. Persons removing to the State with the intention of becoming citizens were required to pay a tax on every slave introduced for the benefit of the State Colonization Society.[41] This act was supplemented by another in 1839. Immigrants were required to make affidavit that it was their intention to become citizens of the State, and to pay a tax on their slaves imported from five to fifteen dollars, according

[38]Laws of Md., 1818, C. 197, Sec. 2.
Dorsey: Vol. I., p. 702.
[39]Laws of Md., 1846, Chap. 340, Sec. 2.
[40]Dorsey: Gen. Public and Private Stat. Law, Vol. II., p. 1069; C. 323, Sec. 4.
[41]Dorsey: Ibid., Vol. I., p. 335, note.
Laws of Gen. Assembly of Md., 1833-4, Chap. 87.

to age.[42] In 1847 a provision was made to allow guardians, executors and trustees residing in the State to bring in slaves appointed by a last will.[43]

In 1850 all laws against the importation of life slaves was repealed except such as extended to those who were slaves for a term of years or those convicted of crime in another State.[44] Maryland continued open to the introduction of slaves.[45]

DELAWARE.

Delaware has the distinction of being the only one of the original Southern States to embody a declaration unfavorable to the importation of slaves in her first constitution. In that of 1776 she says:

"No person hereafter imported into this State from Africa ought to be held in slavery under any pretense whatever; and no negro, Indian,

---

[42]Dorsey: Laws of Md., 1602 to 1839, inclusive, Vol. III., p. 2325. Laws of 1820, Ch. 155.

[43]Laws of Md. 1847, Chap. 232. Sec. 1.

[44]Laws of Md., 1849-50, Chap. 165. Sec. I., II., IV.

[45]Mackall, Md. Code, adopted by Leg. 1860, Vol. I., p. 450.

or mulatto ought to be brought into this State for sale from any part of the world."[46]

In 1787 a law was passed regulating the exportation of slaves. A permit was required to export negroes.[47] A law permitting the introduction of slaves who were devised or inherited was enacted. The law against exportation was made more severe.[48]

In 1793 another law was enacted to further regulate the exportation of slaves. It only made a slight change. Any negro exported contrary to the act was to have his freedom.[49] In 1828 courts were given the right to sentence slaves for certain offenses to be exported. Those thus exported were not allowed to return to the State.[50] There were re-enactments in 1827 and in 1829 concerning the exportation of slaves.[51] In 1833 a law was passed to enable farmers to carry slaves

---

[46]Poore: Fed. and State Constitutions, Part I., p. 277.
[47]Hurd: Vol. II., p. 74.
[48]Ibid., p. 75.
[49]Laws of State of Del., 1793, p. 105-6. This act of Del. was sustained by the Court of Baltimore in a case brought before it in 1840. Liberator, July 24, 1840.
[50]Laws of Delaware, Dover, 1829, Vol. VII., p. 122, Feb. 7, 1829.
[51]Hurd: Vol. II., pp. 79-80.

into Maryland to cultivate land without incurring any penalty.[52]   There seems to have been no more enactments of Delaware concerning importation or exportation of slaves.

LOUISIANA.

The act of Congress in 1804 erecting Louisiana into a territory prohibited the introduction of slaves into it from without the United States. Only slaves imported before May 1, 1798, could be introduced, and those had to be slaves of actual settlers.[53]   An act of Louisiana in 1810 was to prevent the introducing of slaves who had been guilty of crime.[54]

It was not until 1826 that Louisiana as a State passed any law against the introduction of slaves as merchandise.   But this year it was enacted "That no person or persons shall after the first day of June 1826, bring into this State any slave or slaves with the intention to sell or hire the same."   Citizens of Louisiana and immigrants

---

[52]Laws of Del., Vol. VIII., p. 246.   Dover, 1837, passed Feb. 5, 1833.

[53]Poore: Fed. and State Constitutions, Part I., p. 693.

[54]Hurd: Freedom and Bondage, Vol. II., p. 159.

could bring in their own slaves, but were not allowed to hire, exchange or sell them within two
years after such importation.[55] This act was repealed in 1828,[56] but in 1829 another law was
passed which required that any one who should
introduce slaves above twelve years of age to
have a certificate for each slave, signed by two
respectable and well known free-holders of the
county from which the slaves were brought, accompanied with their declaration on oath that
the slaves had never been guilty of crime, and
that they were of good character.   Children under
ten years of age could not be brought in separate
from their mother.[57] This was repealed March 24,
1831.[58]   Almost immediately after the Southampton Massacre in Virginia, Louisiana called
an extra session of her legislature.   The only important act of the session was an act prohibiting
importation of slaves for sale or hire.   Immigrants and citizens were prohibited from bring-

[55]Acts of Second Sess. of Seventh Legislature, pp.
114-116.
[56]Acts 2nd Sess. 8th Leg. (1828), p. 22.
[57]Laws of La., 1829, 1st Sess. 9th Leg., p. 38.
[58]Laws of La., 1831, p. 76.

ing in slaves from Alabama, Mississippi, Florida and Arkansas. Those permitted to be brought in could not be sold or hired within five years. A certificate as in the law of 1829 was also required.[59] It was amended during the same session and the States of Tennessee, Kentucky and Missouri were included in the prohibition.[60]   It was repealed in 1834[61] and no other law with respect to the importation of slaves was ever enacted by Louisiana.

MISSISSIPPI.

The Act of Congress in 1798, establishing a government in the Mississippi Territory prohibited the importation of slaves from without the United States,[62] and the constitution of 1817 excluded slaves guilty of "high crimes in other States."[63]

The territorial act of 1808 made it unlawful

---

[59]Acts of Extra Sess. of 10th Leg. of La., p. 4.

[60]Hurd: Vol. II., p. 162.

[61]Laws of La., 1834, p. 6.

[62]Poore: Fed. and State Constitutions, Part II., p. 1050.

[63]Ibid., p. 1064.

"to expose for sale any slave above fifteen years
of age without having previously exhibited to the
chief justice of the Orphans' Court of the county
where offered for sale, a certificate signed by
two respectable freeholders living in the county
from whence the slave was brought, describing
the stature, complexion, sex, name, and not to
have been guilty of any murder, crime, arson,
burglary, felony, larceny to their knowledge or
belief where he came from, which certificate
shall be signed and acknowledged before the
clerk of the county from whence he came, and
certification by said clerk that those whose names
are prefixed are respectable freeholders.   .   .   .
Such certificates aforesaid shall be registered
with the register of the orphans' court where
such slaves are sold, the seller taking oath that
he believes said certificate is just and true."[64]

In 1819 another act was passed to amend the
law of 1808. Slaves brought into the State as
merchandise were made subject to a tax of twenty
dollars each. A certificate was required as in the

[64]Turner: Statutes of the Miss. Territory, Digested
by Authority of the General Assembly, (1816) p. 386-7.

law of 1808, but it was not to apply to those
brought in for their own use by citizens and immigrants except those from Louisiana and the Alabama territory.[65] An act of 1822 reduced into one
the several acts concerning slaves, free negroes
and mulattoes, but no important changes were
made with regard to the importation of slaves.[66]

The new constitution of 1832, like that of 1817,
excluded slaves guilty of "high crime in other
States." It declared, also, that "The introduction
of slaves into this State as merchandise, or for
sale, shall be prohibited from and after the first
day of May eighteen hundred and thirty-three."[67]

This provision of the constitution gave rise to
a great deal of litigation;[68] nor was it effective in
prohibiting importation of slaves. The latter appears from the fact that in 1837 by an act of the
legislature "the business of introducing or importing slaves into this State as merchandise, or
for sale be, and the same is hereby prohibited."

[65]Acts of 1st Sess. of 2nd Gen. Assem. of Miss., p. 5.
[66]Laws Miss., Adj'd. Sess. June, 1822, p. 179.
[67]Poore: Fed. and State Constitutions, Part II., p.
1077.
[68]De Bow's Review, Vol. VIII., p. 23.

The penalty was $500 and six months' imprison-
ment for each slave so brought in, and notes
which might be given for slaves were not collect-
able.[69]   This law was repealed in 1846.[70]

ALABAMA.

The first law passed by Alabama concerning
the importation of slaves was for the purpose of
carrying into effect the laws of the United
States prohibiting the slave trade.   This was enacted in 1823 and provided that slaves imported
should be employed on public works or sold for
the State.[71]

But on January 13, 1827, it was enacted that
"if any person or persons, shall bring into this
State any slave or slaves, for the purpose of sale
or hire, or shall sell or hire, any slave or slaves
brought into this State after the first day of
August next, such person or persons shall forfeit and pay the sum of $1,000 for each negro
so brought in, one-half thereof to the person suing

---

[69]Laws of Miss. from 1824 to 1838, Pub. by Authority of Legislature, p. 758.

[70]Hurd: Vol. II., p. 148.

[71]Ibid., p. 150.

for the same and the other half to the use of the
State. And, moreover, any person thus offend-
ing shall be subject to indictment, and on conviction shall be liable to be fined a sum not exceeding five hundred dollars for each offense and shall
be imprisoned not exceeding three months, at the
discretion of the jury trying such offense."

Citizens of the State, however, were allowed
to purchase negroes for their own use but could
not sell them until two years after being brought
into the State.[72] This law was repealed in 1829.[73]

Another prohibitive law was passed January
16, 1832. But immigrants were allowed to bring
their own slaves with them and citizens of the
State could import slaves for their own use,
when these introduced slaves returns were to be
made upon oath to the county courts within thirty
days, describing them, and declaring that they
were not introduced for the purpose of sale or
hire. Citizens of Alabama could import slaves
which might have become theirs by inheritance or
marriage. The provisions of the law did not ap-

---

[72]Acts of Assembly of Ala., 1827, p. 44.
[73]Ibid., 1829. p. 63.

ply to travellers, nor to citizens temporarily removed from the State.[74] This was repealed December 4, 1832,[75] and no other prohibitive law was
enacted.

KENTUCKY.

The laws passed by Virginia concerning importation of slaves prior to 1790 were in force in
Kentucky until 1798.[76] This year an act reduc-
ing into one several acts, concerning slaves, free
negroes, mulattoes and Indians was passed. No
slaves could be imported into Kentucky who were
introduced into the United States from foreign
countries, except by immigrants who did not
violate this provision. Citizens could do the same.
But no slaves might be imported as merchandise.[77] An act amending this was approved February 8, 1815. No one was allowed to bring
slaves into Kentucky except those intending to
settle in the State, and they were required to take
the following oath:

---

[74]Acts of Assembly of Ala., 1831-2, pp. 12-13-14.
[75]Ibid., 1832-3, p. 5.
[76]Hurd: Vol. II., pp. 14-15.
[77]Toulmin: A Collection of all the Acts of Ky. now
in Force (1802), pp. 307-308.
　　Hurd: Vol. II., pp. 14-15.

"I, A. B., do swear (or affirm) that my removal
to the State of Kentucky, was with an intention
to become a citizen thereof, and that I have
brought with me no slave or slaves, and will bring
no slave or slaves to this State with the intention
of selling them."[78]

In 1833 it was enacted "That each and every
person who shall hereafter import into this State
any slave or slaves, or who shall sell or buy, or
contract for the sale, or purchase, for a longer
term than one year, of the service of any such
slave or slaves, knowing the same to have been
imported as aforesaid, he, she, or they, so offend-
ing, shall forfeit $600 for each slave so imported,
sold or bought or whose service has been so con-
tracted for."[79]

It was not to apply to immigrants provided they
took the required oath; nor to citizens of Kentucky who derived their "title by will, descent,
distribution, marriage, gift, or in consideration
of marriage;" nor to travellers who could prove

[78]Acts. Leg. 1814-15, pp. 435-6.
[79]Ibid., 1832-33, p. 258.

to the satisfaction of a jury that the slaves were
for necessary attendance.[80]

There were minor acts and quite a number of
acts of a private character.

TENNESSEE.

Tennessee was originally a part of North Carolina and the laws of North Carolina which were in
force at the time of the cession of Tennessee to the
United States in 1790 were continued in force in
Tennessee.[81]

The first law passed by Tennessee with reference to importation of slaves was in 1812.   It
prohibited their importation as merchandise for a
term of five years.   Persons coming as settlers
or residents who had acquired slaves by descent,
devise, marriage, or purchase for their own use
were permitted to import them.   Immigrants
were obliged to take the following oath:

"I, A. B., do solemnly swear or affirm that I
have removed myself and slaves to the State of
Tennessee with the full and sole view of becom-

[80]Laws of Kentucky, 1832-33, p. 258.
[81]Hurd: Vol. II., p. 89 and Note 2.

ing a citizen, and that I have not brought my slave or slaves to this State with any view to the securing of the same against any rebellion or apprehension of rebellion, so help me God."[82]

No other law concerning importation was enacted until 1826. It was practically the same as that of 1812 except that it was a perpetual act and no one was allowed to introduce slaves which had been guilty of crimes in other States.[83] This act continued in force until 1855 when so much of it was repealed as related to the importation of slaves as merchandise.[84]

MISSOURI, ARKANSAS, FLORIDA AND TEXAS.

The Constitution of Missouri (1820) circumscribed the powers of the legislature with reference to importation of slaves as follows:

"The General Assembly shall have no power to pass laws to prevent bona fide immigrants to this State or actual settlers therein from bringing

<hr/>

[82]Acts of Tenn., 2nd Sess., 9th Gen. Assembly (1812), p. 84.

[83]Acts of the Extra Sess. of the 16th General Assembly of Tennessee, 1826, p. 31.

[84]Acts of General Assembly of Tenn., 1855-6, p. 71.

from any of the United States, or from any of their territories, such persons as may there be deemed to be slaves, so long as any persons of the same description are allowed to be held as slaves by the laws of this State.

"They shall have power to pass laws:

"To prohibit the introduction into this State of any slaves who may have committed any high crime in any other State or territory;

"To prohibit the introduction of any slave for the purpose of speculation, or as an article of trade or merchandise;

"To prohibit the introduction of any slave or the offspring of any slave, who heretofore may have been, or who hereafter may be imported from any foreign country into the United States or any territory thereof in contravention of any existing statue of the United States."[85]

The first constitutions of most of the other Southern States had provisions somewhat similar to these among which are Arkansas,[86] Florida,[87] and Texas.[88]

---

[85] Poore: Fed. and State Con., Part II., p. 1107.
[86] Ibid., Part I., p. 113.
[87] Ibid., p. 329.
[88] Ibid., Part II., p. 1779.

The only laws passed by Missouri regarding importation were those of 1835, 1843 and 1845. The law of 1843 simply prohibited the importation of slaves entitled to freedom at a future date[89] and against kidnapping in 1845.[90] The law of 1835 was the leading one. It prohibited the introduction of any slave who had elsewhere committed any infamous crime, or any who had been removed from Missouri for crime, or any imported into the United States contrary to law.[91]

Texas[92] and Florida[93] as States seem never to have prohibited the importation of slaves except those guilty of crime.

The only act of Arkansas concerning importation was passed in 1838 and put in force by proclamation of the Governor March 20, 1839. It was never repealed so far as we could find, and is as follows:

"No person shall knowingly bring or cause to

---

[89]Hurd: Vol. II., p. 170.

[90]Revised Statutes of Mo., Revised and Digested by 13th Gen. Assembly (1844-5). p. 351.

[91]Revised Statutes of Mo. (1844-5), p. 1013.

[92]Hurd: Vol. II., p. 199.

[93]Ibid., p. 192.

be brought into this State, or hold, purchase, hire, sell, or otherwise dispose of within the same; first, any slave who may have committed in any other State, territory or district within the United States, or any foreign country, any offense, which, if committed within the State, would, according to the laws thereof, be felony or infamous crime; or second, any slave who shall have been convicted in this State, of any felony or infamous crime, and ordered to be taken or removed out of this State, according to the laws thereof; or third, any slave who shall have actually been removed out of this State after a conviction of felony or other infamous crime, although no order of removal shall have been made; or fourth, any person or the descendant of any person, who shall have been imported into the United States, or any of the territories thereof in contravention of the laws of the United States, and held as a slave."[94]

[94]English: Digest of Statutes of Arkansas, p. 947, Chap. 154. Sec. 30. Same law in Digest by Gould, pub. 1858, by authority of Legislature, Chap. 162, Sec. 28.

BIBLIOGRAPHY.

Andrews, E. A., Prof.: Slavery and the Domestic
Slave Trade. Boston, 1836.

Adams, Nehemiah: A Southside View of Slavery. Boston, 1854.

Alexander, J. E., Capt.: Transatlantic Sketches,
Comprising Visits to the Most Interesting
Scenes in North America and the West In-
dies.   With Notes on Negro Slavery and
Canadian Emigration.   Philadelphia, 1833.

Ashworth, Henry: A Tour in the United States
and Canada. London (1861.)

Arfwedson, C. D.: The United States and Canada
in 1832, 1833, 1834. 2 vols. London, 1834.

Abdy, E. S.: Journal of a Residence and Tour in
the United States of North America from
April 1833 to October 1834. 3 vols. London,
1835.

American Annual Register for 1827-8-9. (8
vols.) Vol. III. New York, 1835.

An Address to the People of North Carolina on
the Evils of Slavery, by the Friends of
Liberty and Equality. Greensborough, N.
C., 1830, (Y.) Slavery Pamphlets, vol. 61.

Annals of Congress: 8th Congress 1st Session;
9th Congress 2nd Session; 16th Congress
2nd Session.

Annual Report of the American and Foreign
Anti-Slavery Society. 1850.

(Blane, William Newnham) : An Excursion
through the United States and Canada during
the years 1822-23. London, 1824.

Blowe, David: Geographical, Commercial, and
Agricultural View of the United States of
America. Liverpool (1820?)

Buckingham, James Silk. The Eastern and
Western States of America. 3 vol. The
Slave States of America. 2 vol. London,
(1842.)

Bernard, Duke of Saxe-Weimar Eisenach:
Travels through North America during the
years 1825-6. 2 vols. Philadelphia, 1828.

Buxton, Thomas Powell: The African Slave
Trade and Its Remedy. London, 1840.

Birkbeck, Morris: Notes on a Journey in America, from the Coast of Virginia to the Territory of Illinois. Dublin, 1818.

Brinsted, John: The Resources of the United
States of America, or a View of the Agricultural, Commercial, Manufacturing, Financial, Political and Religious Capacity and
Character of the American People.

Basset, John S.: History of Slavery in North
Carolina, J. H. U. Studies. Baltimore, 1899.

Ballaugh, James Curtis: A History of Slavery in
Virginia. Baltimore, 1902.

Brackett, J. R.: The Negro in Maryland. J. H.
U. Studies. Extra volume VI. Baltimore,
1889.

(Candler, Isaac) : A summary view of America;
comprising a description of the face of the
country, and of several of the principal
cities, and remarks on the social, moral and

political character of the people; being the
result of observation and inquiries during a
journey in the United States. London, 1824.

Census of 1890. Vol. Statistics of Agriculture,
p. 42. Washington, D. C.

Census of the United States. Decennial, 1790-
1890. Washington, D. C.

Casey, Charles: Two Years on the Farm of
Uncle Sam: With Sketches of the Location,
Nephews, and Prospects. London, 1852.

Clay, Henry: Colonization Society Speech. Dec.
17, 1829, in African Repository, vol. V.

Carey, H. C.: The Slave Trade, Domestic and
Foreign; Why It Exists, and How It May
Be Extinguished. Philadelphia, 1856.

Chancellor Harper, Governor Hammond, Dr.
Simms, and Professor Dew: The Pro-
Slavery Argument as maintained by the most
distinguished writers of the Southern States.
Philadelphia, 1853. (Charleston, S. C.,
1852).

Chambers, William: American Slavery and Col-
our. London, 1857.

Child, Mrs.: Anti-Slavery Catechism, Second
Edition, Newburyport, 1839. (Yale) Slavery Pamphlets, vol. 62.

Chase, Henry, and Chas. W. Sanborn: The North
and the South. Boston, 1856.

Claiborne, J. F. H.: Mississippi as a Province,
Territory and State, with Biographical No-
tice of Eminent Citizens. Vol. I. Jackson,
Miss., 1880.

De Bow, J. D. B.: The Industrial Resources of
the Southern and Western States; Embrac-

ing a View of their Commerce, Agriculture, Manufactures, Internal Improvements, Slave and Free Labor, Slavery Institutions, Products, etc., of the South.   3 vols.   New Orleans, 1853.

Compendium of Seventh Census (1850). Washington, 1854.

Du Bois, W. E. Burghardt: The Suppression of the African Slave Trade to the United States of America.   (1638-1870.)   New York, 1896.

Du Bois, W. E. B.: The Enforcement of the Slave Trade Laws.   Annual Report of the American Historical Association for the year 1891, p. 163.   Washington, 1892.

Darby, William: The Emigrant's Guide to the Western and Southwestern States and Territories.   New York, 1818.

Darby, William: A Geographical Description of the State of Louisiana; presenting a View of the Soil, Climate, Animal, Vegetable and Mineral Productions, . . . with an Account of the Character and Manners of the Inhabitants. . . . Philadelphia, 1816.

Duncan, John M.; A. B.: Travels Through the U. S. and Canada in 1819. 2 vols. N. Y., 1823.

Dew, Thomas: Review of the Debate in the Virginia Assembly of 1831-32. (Yale) Slavery Pamphlets, vol. 42.

Evans, Estwick: A Pedestrious Tour of Four Thousand Miles, through the Western States and Territories, during the Winter and Spring of 1818.   Concord, N. H., 1819.

Edwards, Byron: History, Civil and Commercial,

of the British Colonies of the West Indies.
3 vols. London, 1807.

Fearon, Henry Bradshaw: Sketches of America.
(Second Ed.) London, 1818.

Featherstonhaugh, G. W.: An Excursion
Through the Slavery States. 2 vols. London, 1844.

Flint, Timothy: The History and Geography of
the Mississippi Valley. 2 vols. (3rd ed.)
Cincinnati and Boston, 1833.

Facts Respecting Slavery. (Yale.) Slavery
Pamphlets, vol. 61.

Ford, Paul Leicester: The Writings of Thomas
Jefferson. Collected and Edited. 10 vols.
New York, 1892-1899.

Finch, J.: Travels in the United States of America and Canada. London, 1833.

Faux, W.: Memorable Days in America; being
a Journal of a Tour to the United States,
principally undertaken to ascertain by positive Evidence, the Condition and Probable
Prospects of British Emigrants. London,
1823.

Gales and Seaton's Register of Debates in Congress, vol. V. Washington, D. C.

Hall, Captain Basil: Travels in North America in
the years 1827 and 1828. 2 vols.

Hall, Francis: Travels in Canada and the United
States. (In 1816 and 1817). London, 1818.

Hodgson, Adams: Letters from North America,
written during a Tour of the United States
and Canada. 2 vols. London, 1824.

Holmes, Isaac: An Account of the United States
of America, Derived from Actual Observa-

tion, During a Residence of Four Years in that Republic. London (1823).

Hammond, M. B.: The Cotton Industry. An Essay in American Economic History. Part I. New York, 1897.

Helps, Sir Arthur: Spanish Conquest in America. 3 vols. London, 1856.

Howison, R. R.: History of Virginia, 2 vols. Richmond, 1848.

Helper, Hinton Rowan: The Impending Crisis of the South; How to Meet It. New York, 1857.

(Ingraham, J. H.): The Southwest, 2 vols. (by a Yankee). New York, 1835.

Jay, William: A View of the Action of the Federal Government in Behalf of Slavery. New York, 1839.
Miscellaneous Writings on Slavery. Boston and London, 1853.

(Knight, H. C.) Arthur Singleton: Letters from the South and West. Boston, 1824.

Kemble, F. A.: Journal of a Residence on a Georgian Plantation in 1838-9. N. Y. 1863.

Lalor, John J.: Editor Cyclopœdia of Political Science, Political Economy and the History of the United States by the Best American and European Writers. 3 vols. Chicago, 1881.

Locke, Mary Sloughton: Anti-Slavery in America from the Introduction of African Slaves to the Prohibition of the Slave Trade. (1619-1808.) Boston, 1901.

Lewis, Rev. G.: Impressions of America and the American Churches. Edinburgh, 1845.

Letter from the Secretary of the Treasury, Trans-
mitting Information Relating to the Illicit
Introduction of Slaves Into the United
States. First Session, 16th Congress.
House Document (42). Washington, 1820.

Letter from the Secretary of the Navy, Transmit-
ting Copies of Instructions which have been
issued to Naval Commanders upon the Subject of the Importation of Slaves, made in
pursuance of a Resolution of the House of
Representatives of the 4th of January In-
stant. State Papers 2nd Session 15th Congress. IV. Doc. 84. Washington, 1819.

Monette, John W.: History of the Discovery and
Settlement of the Valley of the Mississippi by
Spain, France and Great Britain, and the
Subsequent Occupation, Settlement and Ex-
tension of Civil Government by the United
States until the year 1846. Vol. II. New
York, 1846.

Morse, P. A.: Southern Slavery and the Cotton
Trade. De Bow's Review, vol. XXIII. New
Orleans and Washington City, 1857.

Martineau, Harriet: Retrospect of Western
Travel. 3 vols. London, 1838.
Society in America. 3 vols. London, 1837.

Marshall, Thomas: Speech in the Virginia
House of Delegates, 1832. Richmond Enquirer, Feb. 2, 1832.

M'Call, Hugh: History of Georgia. Savannah,
Ga. 1811.

Melish, John: A Geographical Description of the
United States. New York, 1826.

Murray, Charles Augustus: Travels in North

America, during the years 1834-5-6.   New York, 1839.

Nolte, Vincent: Fifty Years in Both Hemispheres.   Reminiscence of the Life of a Former Merchant.   Translated from the German.   New York, 1854.

Olmsted, Frederick Law: A Journey in the Seaboard Slave States, with Remarks on Their Economy.   New York, 1856.

A Journey in the Back Country.   New York, 1860.

The Cotton Kingdom: A Traveller's Observations on Cotton and Slavery in the American Slave States.   2 vols.   New York, 1862.

(Paulding, James Kirk):   Letters from the South during an Excursion in 1816.   2 vols.   New York, 1817.

Proceedings and Debates of the Virginia State Convention, 1829-30.   Richmond, 1830.

Prospects of the Rubicon.   (Yale).   Slavery Pamphlets, vol. 48.   Philadelphia, 1832.

Palmer, John: Journal of Travels in the United States of North America, and in Lower Canada, performed in the year 1817; containing Particulars Relating to the Prices of Land and Provisions, Remarks on the Country and People, etc.   London, 1818.

Poore, Ben. Perley: The Federal and State Constitutions, Colonial Charters and Organic Laws of the United States.   2 vols.   Washington, 1878.   2nd Ed.

Reed, Andrew, D. D., and James Matheson, D.D.:   A Narrative of a Visit to the American Churches.   Deputation from the Congregational Union of England and Wales. 2 vols. New York, 1835.

Rankin, John: Letters on American Slavery Addressed to Thomas Rankin, Middlebrook, Va. Fifth edition. Boston, 1838.

Rhodes, James Ford: History of the United States from the Compromise of 1850. 4 vols. New York, 1893-1899.

Shaffner, Colonel Tal. P.: The War in America; being an Historical and Political Account of the Southern and Northern States. London (1862).

Slavery and the Internal Slave Trade in North America: Answers to Queries, Transmitted by the Committee of the British and Foreign Anti-Slavery Society. Presented to the General Anti-Slavery Convention held in London, 1840. London, 1841.

Stowe, Harriet Beecher: A Key to Uncle Tom's Cabin; presenting the Original Facts and Documents upon which the Story is Founded. Boston, 1853.

Scharf, J. Thomas: History of Maryland from the Earliest Period to the Present Day. 3 vols. Baltimore, 1879.

Sequel to Mrs. Kemble's Journal. (Yale.) Slavery Pamphlets, vol. 17.

Stearns, Edward Josiah: Notes on Uncle Tom's Cabin; being a Logical Answer to Its Allegations and Inferences Against Slavery as an Institution. 2nd Ed. Philadelphia, 1853.

Stuart, James: Three Years in North America. 2 vols. Edinburgh, 1833.

Sturge, Joseph: A Visit to the United States in 1841. Boston, 1842.

Scutz, Christian: Travels on An Inland Voyage Through the States of New York, Pennsylvania, Virginia, Ohio, Kentucky and Tennessee, and Through the Territories of Indiana, Louisiana, Mississippi and New Orleans in the years 1807 and 1808. 2 vols. New York, 1810.

Smedes, Susan Dabney: Memorials of a Southern Planter. Baltimore, 1887.

Siebert, Wilber: The Underground Railroad from Slavery to Freedom. New York, 1898.

Schouler, James: History of the United States of America under the Constitution. 6 vols. Washington, D. C., 1880-1899.

Smith, Capt. John: General History. 2 vols. Richmond, 1819.

Saunders, William L.: The Colonial Records of North Carolina. Vols. I. II. V. Raleigh, 1886.

Torrey, Jessie: A Portraiture of Domestic Slavery in the United States, including Memoirs of Facts on the Interior Traffic in Slaves and on Kidnapping. Philadelphia, 1817.

Turnbull, David: Travels in the West, Cuba; with Notices of Porto Rico and the Slave Trade. London, 1840.

Tower, Philo, Rev.: Slavery Unmasked; Being a Truthful Narrative of a Three Years' Residence in Eleven Southern States. Rochester, N. Y., 1856.

Tremain, Mary: Slavery in the District of Columbia, the Policy of Congress and the

Struggle for Abolition. University of Ne-
braska, Seminary Papers, Number 2. New
York, 1892.

Vigne, Godfrey T.: Six Months in America.
Philadelphia, 1833.

Van Evrie, John H.: Negroes and Negro
"Slavery"; the first an inferior race; the
Latter its normal condition. New York,
1861.

Woodbury, Levi (Secretary of the Treasury):
Report of the Cotton Production and Con-
sumption of the United States. Executive
Document, First Session, 24th Congress.
No. 146. 1836.

Wright, Frances: Views of Society and Manners
in America. New York, 1821; London,
1822.

Worty, Lady Emmeline Stuart: Travels in
United States. 1849-50. New York, 1851.

Weld, Charles Richard: A Vacation Tour of the
United States and Canada. London, 1855.

Weston, G. M.: The Progress of Slavery in the
United States. Washington, 1857.

Whittier, John G.: A Letter in the "Emancipator," Nov. 23, 1843.

PERIODICALS AND NEWSPAPERS.

Quarterly, Anti-Slavery Magazine. Vol. II.
New York, 1837.

De Bow's Review, New Orleans. 1846-1861,
especially vols. 3, 8, 18, 22, 23, 24 and 26.

The African Repository and Colonial Journal.
Vol. V., 1830, Washington.

Charleston Courier. Charleston, S. C. 1835.

Cambridge Chronicle, Cambridge, Md. 1831.

The Christian Citizen, Worcester and Boston,
1844.

Christian Freeman, Hartford, Conn. 1845.

Charleston Mercury, Charleston, S. C. 1833.

The Emancipator, New York. 1842, 1843, 1848.

Richmond Enquirer, Richmond, 1831, 1832, 1859.

Village Herald, Princess Anne, Md. 1831.

The Virginia Herald, Fredericksburg, Va. 1836.

Winyaw Intelligencer, Georgeton, S. C. 1830.

The Liberator, (Wm. L. Garrison, Ed.) 1831-
1861.

The Mississippian; Jackson, Miss. 1837.

Snow Hill Messenger and Worcester County
Advertiser, Snow Hill, Md. 1832, 1833.

Freeman Hunt: The Merchants' Magazine and
Commercial Review.   Vols. VI., XV.,
XLIII. New York.

The National Era, Washington. 1847, 1849.

Daily National Intelligencer, Washington, D. C.
1836.

Niles' Register, Baltimore, Md.   1812-1861,
especially 1817, 1818, 1820, 1824, 1826, 1828,
1829, 1831.

Norfolk and Portsmouth Herald. Norfolk, Va.
1826.

New Orleans Picayune, New Orleans, 1846, 1856,
1858, 1859.

North Carolina Standard, Raleigh, N. C. 1837.

LAWS.

Alabama:
Act of the General Assembly of 1827, 1831-2, 1832-3, 1840-41.

Arkansas:
A Digest of the Statutes of Arkansas embracing all laws of a general and Permanent Character in Force at the close of the Session of the General Assembly of 1846. Little Rock, Ark. 1848.

Delaware:
Laws of 1793; 1829, in Vol. VII.; 1833 in Vol. VIII.

Florida:
Laws of 1850-51.

Georgia:
Acts of the General Assembly of 1817, 1824, 1835, 1849-50, 1855-6.
Oliver H. Prince: A Digest of the Laws of Georgia in force December, 1837. By Authority of the Legislature. Athens, Ga. 1837.

Kentucky:
Laws of 1814-15, 1832-33.
Harry Toulmin: A Collection of all Public and Permanent Acts of the General Assembly of Kentucky which are now in Force. Frankford, Ky. 1802.

Louisiana:
Laws of 1826, 1828, 1829, 1831, (also Extra Sess. 1831). 1834.

Maryland:

Laws of 1809, 1818, 1833-4, 1846, 1847, 1849-50.

Clement Dorsey: The General Public Statutory Law and Public Local Law of the State of Maryland from the year 1692 to 1836 inclusive. 3 vols. Baltimore, 1840.

Virgil Maxcy: The Revised Laws of Maryland. 3 vols. Baltimore. 1811.

Henry C. Mackall: The Maryland Code Adopted by the Legislature in 1860. Baltimore, 1860.

Mississippi:

Laws . . . from January Session 1824 to the January Session 1838 inclusive. Published by Authority of the Legislature. Jackson, Miss. 1838.

Laws of 1819. Adjd. Sess. 1822.

(Turner): Statutes of the Mississippi Territory, Digested by authority of the General Assembly. Natchez, 1816.

A. Hutchinson: Code of Mississippi from 1798 to 1848. Jackson, 1848.

Missouri:

Laws of the State of Missouri. Revised and Digested by Authority of the General Assembly. 2 vols. St. Louis, 1825.

Revised Statutes of the State of Missouri. Revised and Digested by the 13th General Assembly, Session 1844-5. St. Louis, 1845.

North Carolina:

Laws of the State of North Carolina as are now in Force in this State. Revised under Authority of the General Assembly of 1819. 2 vols. Raleigh, 1821.

Revised Statutes passed by the General Assembly
of 1836-7. 2 vols. Raleigh, 1837.
John Haywood: A Manual of the Laws of North
Carolina; (4th Ed.) Raleigh, 1819.

South Carolina:
Laws of 1816, 1817, 1818, 1823, 1835, 1837, 1847,
1848.
Acts of the General Assembly of the State of
South Carolina from February 1791 to De-
cember 1794, both inclusive. 1st vol. 1795 to
1804, both inclusive. Columbia, 1808.
David J. McCord: The Statutes at Large of
South Carolina. Edited under Authority of
the Legislature. Vol. VII. Columbia, 1840.

Tennessee:
Laws of 1812, Extra Sess. 1826, 1855.

Virginia:
Acts of the General Assembly of 1810-11, 1818-
19.
Samuel Shepherd: The Statutes at Large of Vir-
ginia, from October Session 1792 to Decem-
ber Session 1806 inclusive. 3 vols. (New
Series). Being a continuation of Hening.
Richmond, 1835 and 1836.
Wm. Waller Hening: Statutes at Large of Vir-
ginia. 13 vols. Richmond, 1812.
United States, Statutes at Large Vol. V.
T. R. R. Cobb: Law of Negro Slavery in the
Various States of the United States. Phila-
delphia, 1856.
John Codman Hurd: The Law of Freedom and
Bondage in the United States. 2 vols. Bos-
ton, 1862.